A TRAINING MANUAL FOR SMALL GROUP LEADERS

A TRAINING MANUAL FOR SMALL GROUP LEADERS

JULIE A. GORMAN

VICTOR BOOKS®

A DIVISION OF SCRIPTURE PRESS PUBLICATIONS INC.
USA CANADA ENGLAND

Most Scripture quotations are from the *Holy Bible, New International Version,* © 1973, 1978, 1984, International Bible Society. Used by permission of Zondervan Bible Publishers.

Library of Congress Cataloging-in-Publication Data

Gorman, Julie A.
A training manual for small group leaders / by Julie A.
Gorman.
    p.   cm.–(GroupBuilder resources)
    ISBN 0-89693-266-4
    1. Church   group   work — Handbooks,   manuals,
etc. I. Title. II. Series.
BV652.2.G58   1991
253.7–dc20   91-18688
                                                CIP

1 2 3 4 5 6 7 8 9 10 Printing / Year 95 94 93 92 91

CONTENTS

89517

How to Use This Training Manual

Wanted: Small Group Leaders. If you're looking at this manual, you realize that effective small group leaders are made, not born. The well-equipped small group leader needs to:

▶ Understand the dynamics of personal growth.
▶ Develop people skills.
▶ Encourage changes in behavior and attitude.
▶ Utilize principles of group dynamics.
▶ Feel good about his or her ministry.
▶ Become adept at helping group members relate and grow together.

This means that it will not be enough for persons to "go through another class" or "read another book." What you are after is individual change which leads to life-changing groups. The sessions in this manual have been designed with this goal in mind.

What You'll Need. To use this manual you need two things: (1) a group of new or experienced leaders with a desire to grow, and (2) a **Trainer/Facilitator** for each session. If you're an experienced small group leader, or Christian educator, you may want to act as the **Trainer** for each of the eight sessions. However, these sessions are not dependent on "expert" leadership. As an alternative, you may want to take turns leading the sessions, giving group members an opportunity for some practical experience.

What Will Happen. The overall plan for these equipping sessions will move participants from questions to answers, from problems to solutions, from concerns to doing something about those concerns, from perfunctorily following directions to understanding underlying reasons and purposes. Before a person receives new ideas, that person must be made aware of the need for change. For example, advertisers create a market by showing people what they are missing. They continually bombard us with messages about what is lacking with our present VCR ("You need that extra feature"), car ("You could be getting more miles per gallon"), or life ("You only live once"). This heightening of awareness is motivating because we all "want something better." Equipping must do the same. People will not go through the process of change unless they need it and are motivated to pursue what is necessary for change. Too often we just give them information, expecting that they know they need to change.

Identifying the Issue, the first section of each session, is the key that opens the door to learning and change. You will find provocative stimulators in this section which are meant to help participants ask questions or realize a need they or their group members face.

This focused motivation leads into an information section called **Exploring An Idea.** The emphasis here is on providing ideas and questions that will help resolve the issue. Your job as **Trainer** is to make clear new insights, showing how they will enrich or strengthen the group. But knowing what to do and even how to do it doesn't mean that small group leaders will automatically put into practice new insights. To strengthen the actual use of an idea requires the third section called **Experiencing the Insight.** Here is where your equipping time will win or lose. The more you can help small group leaders reframe new ideas into existing situations or actual group plans, the more likely they will be to carry out changed behaviors. Educators have shown that ideas transfer into actions when learners experience what the idea is like in practice. Plan carefully for this last section. Leave enough time to carry out what you have taught. Adapt the suggested experiences so they fit your group's situation. Use illustrations and actual happenings from your small groups so the new ideas become familiar and seem to "fit." Cause information to "come alive" by making it personal and specific. Don't settle for anything less than equipping your small group leaders for ministry.

SOME NOTES TO THE TRAINER

What to Expect of This Manual. First, you can plan on more than information. These sessions are *formation* centered. Each teaching/learning opportunity is designed to re-form attitudes, not just skills and insights. To achieve this, the sessions have been deliberately designed to give participants time to work through values as well as ideas. People need time to get in touch with why each operates as he does. These materials purposefully ask for personalizing of concepts so each person discovers what the idea means to her. Unless a person understands a concept in terms of her already constructed sphere of operations, there will be no integration or change. Therefore, the session **Trainer** should accent the importance of this by allowing ample time for participants to share with each other on suggestions that ask "Share a time when you experienced . . ." or urge, "Let's try it out." Experiencing an idea leads to change more than simply hearing it proclaimed with a "should" or an "ought to do."

Plan on Experiential Activities. Experiencing takes more time than telling. Processing takes more time than hearing. Simply telling a leader what to do has not proved effective in most cases in long-term change of leadership style. Plan your schedule with enough time for group members to experience what you are teaching them. Take care to adjust the simulated or real activities so that they fit the situations of your group for maximum learning. Most learning occurs where learners get involved with more than one sense, not just hearing, not just seeing, but responding verbally as well as formulating a plan and taking responsibility for acting on an issue.

Create a Climate for Change. Change more readily occurs when the simulated situation is much like the real situation where you desire the skill or attitude to be practiced. Therefore, if you can meet in a setting similar to the small group one experienced by your leaders (perhaps a home, in a living room area, around a table, etc.), you will likely have greater transfer of skills. By requiring leaders to learn and practice in small group formats, they are likely to carry over to their own groups what is emphasized in each equipping session. Persons can copy what is done even if they can't verbalize why.

Demonstrate How It's Done. Modeling how to do a skill reinforces the verbal with the visual and heightens learning. Some people learn by picturing an action taking place. These visual learners recall what was seen and heard and duplicate what they've observed. This is particularly true of skill development, whether it be knot tying or evangelism training.

Make Use of What a Group Member Already Knows. When equipping adults we seldom start from scratch. Somewhere in their experience is a model or a mind-set that is recalled when action is required. The sum of those experiences gives an adult a sense of competence and worth as a person who "knows." While some of their previous information and experience may prove faulty, none of it can be ignored by the one seeking to equip with new attitudes and patterns of operation. When a new concept is internalized and integrated with what is already known by a learner, the bridge is made from the new insight in the learning session to the familiar setting of the leader's group. If we want leaders not just to go through equipping sessions but to be transformed by them, we will work on being aware of what they already know and do and tie in new ideas with these established insights. Work at finding out what people know and then choose activities to which you and your group can relate.

Small Groups Are the People of God in Action. In many ways small groups give opportunity for persons to "be the people of God in action." Each of the equipping sessions that follow bears this in mind. Every leader must be nurtured in his or her own life and grasp that the small group leader's role is more than a position to be filled—it is a mission to fulfill the will of God in both leader's and group members' lives. God's

10

people must be released to be the church and equipped to fulfill their calling. Experiencing the biblical portions of these learning sessions is vital to the grasp of skills and to the motivation and support to "pastor a people" who are in the process of transformation. Each equipping session deliberately gives time to focus on some biblical insight related to the topic. Our Divine Equipper gives insight into not only the content but also the process of transformation of the believer. Enabling persons to grow in community is not a humanistic idea—it was God's original plan. The biblical emphasis reminds us of our spiritual heritage and destiny.

EQUIPPING SESSION 1

OFF TO A GOOD START
How to Plan your First
Small Group Meeting

. . . .

TARGET

By the end of this session you will:

▶ Understand and feel secure in what they will do the first time your group is together.
▶ Realize the importance of the first meeting.
▶ Learn practical ways to achieve your goals.
▶ Make a commitment to follow through on this methodology at the first meeting.
▶ Experience for yourselves what you will help others experience.

MATERIALS NEEDED

Name tags (if your group leaders don't know each other)
Moveable chairs

Overhead projector

Blank transparencies, chalkboard, or newsprint for recording responses

IDENTIFYING THE ISSUE

The aim for this part of the session is to help group leaders know and experience what group members need and feel like when the group comes together for the first time. The major emphases in this session and those of the first small group session are:

▶ Build a sense of security by getting acquainted (trading personal information). This is accomplished by structuring the setting for care and belonging and by giving information that informs and makes aware.

▶ Build a sense of "I'm important and included" by allowing everyone to share expectations and by inviting all to become highly involved.

▶ Build a sense of ownership by sharing responsibilities and by asking group members to commit and invest themselves in the group.

"Who Are You?" Divide into three's or four's. If you don't know each other, begin by completing the following statements.

> **My name is. . . .**
> **I am a person interested in small groups because. . . .**
> **One thing I want to learn is. . . .**

Note how this little bit of information and interaction helps everyone feel more comfortable. Allow a few minutes to discuss each question. Then share some of the highlights of your discussions.

"What Are You Like in New Circumstances?" Think of your

14

first time in a new place: a class in which you've enrolled, a new church you visit, starting a new job, going on a first date, going to camp for the first time. Think about how you feel, what you fear. How do you respond to this new situation? What thoughts run through your mind? Make a list of these.

Identify feelings underlying the statements you've collected. What feelings accompany a person's first experience in a new group?

```
┌──────────────────── Trainer's Notes ────────────────────┐
│                                                          │
│  Suggest some of the following answers to get the group  │
│  leaders started:                                        │
│                                                          │
│      I'm curious, but cautious.   What's expected of me? │
│      I don't know what to do.     Where do I go?         │
│      I'm open, but guarded.       Will I like it here?   │
│      What's going on?             Will I like these people? │
│      Can I trust this group?      Will they like me?     │
│      Anticipation                 Excitement Anxiety     │
│      Insecurity                   Fear                   │
│      Inhibition of freedom        Tension                │
│                                                          │
└──────────────────────────────────────────────────────────┘
```

EXPLORING AN IDEA
When most people experience something new, their greatest need is to feel secure. They can't relax and get something out

of what is going on—be themselves—unless there is security. Security building helps take away fear and anxiety and grants a person a greater feeling of freedom.

"What Builds a Sense of Security?" Think back again to that first-time experience you just recalled. What kinds of things helped or would have helped you feel more secure in that situation? As you suggest answers to these questions, discuss the implications for your small group's first time together.

Trainer's Notes

To keep the discussion going, you might want to suggest some of the following "security builders":

▶ Getting to know somebody.
▶ Somebody knowing my name.
▶ Finding a 'place' for me.
▶ Sensing that somebody's in charge and knows what's going on.
▶ Giving me information so I knew what was happening.
▶ Treating me as valuable and special.

Trading Personal Information. Sharing stories about personal incidents is a safe way to trade a piece of yourself for a piece of another person. As long as the information is not threatening, giving information about yourself is an excellent "security builder." However, careful attention must be given to the type of information you ask your group members to share. Asking group members the question "What do you do?" can threaten and divide the group as persons identify with different "levels" of jobs. In this case, going around the room and introducing yourselves may become a status show or power play. A better approach might be to ask each member for two descriptive words that describe how he sees himself. Titles may impress but also divide. What other kinds of information make people feel they know and can relate to another?

At this first stage of your small group's development, ask members to share "happenings" rather than beliefs and convictions. Ask not only for facts, but for feelings about those facts if you really want people to feel accepting of one another. Sharing how you feel about your hometown is more insightful than "Where were you born?"

The more persons in your group know about each other, the greater will be the trust. What guidelines does this suggest for you as your group meets for the first time?

Trainer's Notes

Suggest the following guidelines to aid the discussion:

▶ Come prepared with good questions.
▶ Plan for group members to do most of the talking.
▶ Allow time for "group building" right from the start.

As you build trust, the depth of your discussions will also increase. To aid this process, it is important to remember this simple rule: the more intimate the topic, the smaller the group with whom it is shared. It is easier to share feelings and concerns with two or three persons, so match the question with the size of group required. Which of these questions would you place in a small unit for sharing?

▶ What is a small group experience that you cherish?
▶ What did you want to be when you were ten and why?
▶ How did you feel about God in your teenage years?
▶ What was your placement in your family (e.g., firstborn) and how did you feel about it?

▶ What descriptive words come to mind when you think of small groups?

▶ What were two important factors in your coming to know Jesus?

Another factor impacting your decision to select a large or small unit is the amount of time required to answer the question and the cumulative time this would require of your small group. Offsetting this is the number of persons who will be "built together" upon hearing another's story. Sometimes, to build a sense of "whole group," time should be given for the larger group to hear each individual's story.

Regardless of these choices, make the sharing of personal information a priority for your first group session. It is vital to "build people to people" before beginning any kind of study or asking for ideas. Knowing another builds trust and causes a person to feel safer when it comes to sharing ideas. If this trust is not established, sharing is inhibited by a member's fear that her ideas will be rejected. And in the setting of a first session, that means personal rejection. Without trust, some members may become closed and defensive, presenting a contrary idea just to "top" another, or criticizing another's suggestion to prove personal importance.

Trainer's Notes
Draw your group leaders' attention to the following seating plan. In groups of four, have group leaders discuss the seating plan using the questions below. Allow 10 minutes for discussion.

Seating Plans

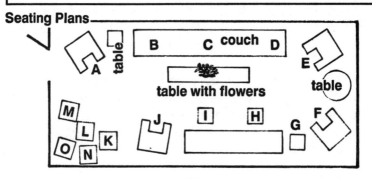

Structure a Secure Setting. Discuss the seating plan in the diagram using these questions as a guide.

1. Where should the group leader sit to make people feel secure? Why?

2. Where should coleaders sit? Why?

3. Which chairs are likely to be filled first? Last? Who is likely to feel "out of it"?

4. What would you change to help people feel more secure in this setting? Why?

5. What happens to **C** when the group divides into smaller discussion groups?

6. Which persons, because of where they are seated, are likely to be quiet during discussion?

7. Suppose four chairs are empty and can be removed. Which four would you remove to take away the "emptiness" of an incomplete circle?

8. What are some important guidelines about seating for creating a good group?

If needed, suggest some of the following possible answers to aid your discussion:

1. Probably **E** so he or she can be seen by all.
2. It's best for coleaders to divide up to infiltrate
   group with warmth. Sit by a quiet person or new
   member.
3. **H** will probably be filled last, **I** first.
6. **G, K, L, N,** and **O** will be the quiet chairs in this
   session.
7. Get rid of **H, I, N,** and **O,** or pull **G,** out and move
   K, L, and **M** toward **A** and **A** toward **B.**
8. All need to see each other. No one should be stuck
   out in front or behind. Everybody needs to be beside a person to whom he or she can talk.

Sharing Expectations. Giving and receiving information helps a
person feel secure and causes each to feel a sense of belonging. As you think of leading your first group meeting, you're
probably wondering, "What's expected of me?" Your group
members will be asking themselves the same question.
That's why discussing program details and established facts
along with hopes and desires is very important. The more
members are aware of assumptions, the more they will feel
included.

Some expectations are shared in words: "We plan to have a
potluck each time with everyone bringing something." Some
information is presented by our actions. For instance, you tell
group members how much you want them included by the
way you lead. These expectations are unspoken but read
clearly by participants. What expectations have been commu-
nicated by the way this first training session is being lead?
Are you hearing: "We work as a team and like to include
everybody. We value your input. We want to know who you
are and what you know."

As a leader, it's important that you spell out what is important to you and why. For example, "Your strongest vote is

your presence. Absence means we are not whole and we have to start over to build relationships." Or "We expect that every member will participate in this group—sharing your ideas and questions, helping to set up socials, listening to one another as you see somebody needing a listening ear or a phone call or lunch time."

Get with another small group leader and share one assumption that is important to you as you begin your small group.

One assumption that is important to me as I begin my small group is . . . .

Along with sharing your expectations, you will want to discover your group members' intentions. Asking questions and promoting dialogue help you find out how much commitment you can expect—what members intend to put into the group, what they hope to get out of it. You might try these questions:

▶ What's one thing you would really like to get out of this group?
▶ What would we need to do in order for that to happen?
▶ What helps you feel cared for? A way you enjoy expressing care?
▶ How much energy can we put forth in this group? High level of time and effort? Minimal effort because of other commitments?
▶ What would you like this group to be in order to be satisfying for you?
▶ What's one thing you don't want in this group?

EXPERIENCING THE INSIGHT

In groups of three or four discuss the following checklist. List one thing you plan to include in your first group session because of its importance to you.

Suggest that group leaders use the following Planning Checklist to plan their first small group session.

Planning Your First Session

Check YES for any of the following activities you would consider including in your small group's first session, NO for activities you would not include. As a group, discuss the reasons for your answers.

At the first meeting, do I begin: **YES / NO**

1. By handing out a Bible knowledge questionnaire?
2. With a meal?
3. By asking each person to share an area where he or she needs to grow?
4. By asking group members to share their previous small group experience and what they liked or disliked about it?
5. By reading my list of expectations and group rules to them?
6. By handing out a schedule of planned group sessions?
7. With an activity in which people get to know each other's names and one thing about each other?

What other planned activities do you want to include in your first meeting? Circle those you want to include and add any others at the end of this list.

Social time
Self-descriptive sharing
Going over materials
Talking about the kind
of group you want

Hand out written information
One-to-one times
Informal sharing
Sharing in 3s or 4s

Large group share time	Singing
Ask for their vision for group	Prayer
	Divide into partners for follow-up
Share expectations	Set goals
Plan a social get-together	
Play a get-acquainted game	Make nametags
	Take a group picture
Collect addresses	Collect birthdates

So What Kind of Leader Is Needed at the First Meeting? Listed below are leader attitudes that are important, especially for the first meeting of the group. What actions would you suggest to express each attitude?

Leader's Attitudes	Leader's Actions
Warmth	
Caring	
Aware of tensions	
Confident, but relaxed	
Valuing of others	
Sensitive	

A Basis for Real Security. How has God given each of us as His children a sense of security? The psalmist says, "O Lord, You have searched me and You know me," but that knowledge is not disconcerting to him. In fact, he trusts God so deeply that he invites, "Search me, O God, and know my heart; test me and know my anxious thoughts" (Ps. 139:23). God had so revealed Himself to David that David felt at home in trusting God. What is one thing special that God has revealed to you about Himself that gives you a sense of being able to trust Him?

23

Psalm 91:1-2 declares, "He who dwells in the shelter of the Most High will rest in the shadow of the Almighty. I will say of the Lord, 'He is my refuge and my fortress, my God, in whom I trust.' " What does God do that cultivates a sense of security in you?

As a small group leader, it is a great assurance to know that Jesus has called you to be His, to serve His family in love. And He who has called us is the Faithful One. Commit yourself to this Faithful Leader who will work His works in you and through you as you lead. Pair up and pray for each other.

EQUIPPING SESSION 2

LAY A STRONG FOUNDATION
How to Create a Covenant

∙∙∙

TARGET
By the end of this session you will:

▶ Know the purpose for every group member having a shared understanding.
▶ Be motivated to develop a contract.
▶ Know how to design a covenant.
▶ Think through your own expectations and responsibilities.
▶ Create a statement or contract that includes your expectations and responsibilities.

MATERIALS NEEDED
Moveable chairs
Overhead projector
Blank transparencies, chalkboard, or newsprint for recording responses

IDENTIFYING THE ISSUE

Divide into groups of four to take a look at 2 Chronicles 7:13-14, 17-18 which illustrates a biblical covenant. See what can be discovered about covenants from these examples.

¹³"When I shut up the heavens so that there is no rain, or command locusts to devour the land or send a plague among My people, ¹⁴if My people, who are called by My name, will humble themselves and pray and seek My face and turn from their wicked ways, then will I hear from heaven and will forgive their sin and will heal their land. . . .

¹⁷"As for you, if you walk before Me as David your father did, and do all I command, and observe My decrees and laws, ¹⁸I will establish your royal throne, as I covenanted with David your father when I said, 'You shall never fail to have a man to rule over Israel.' "

2 Chronicles 7:13-14, 17-18

Trainer's Notes

Suggest some of the following discoveries to get the discussion going: Covenants take at least two parties, need to be expressed verbally, share expectations, involve privilege and responsibility, mean commitment to promises not yet fulfilled.

How many different kinds of contracts, covenants, or agreements are a part of your life right now? (rental contract, house mortgage, auto loan, insurance, marriage, etc.).

Covenant may be defined as "a shared understanding of expectations and responsibilities." What do you consider to be a key word in this definition and why?

An Experience of Shared Understanding. Imagine that you and the other small group leaders in your foursome are going to buy a new car together. But you need to work through what you want. Each of you is putting in an equal amount so each has an equal say. Take 10 minutes to decide, as a group, what you will say to the salesperson who will write up your order.

```
┌──────────────── Trainer's Notes ────────────────┐
│                                                   │
│  After 10 minutes, reassemble the group leaders   │
│  and discuss the questions below. Depending on    │
│  your time schedule, you may or may not want      │
│  groups to share what they have decided.          │
│                                                   │
└───────────────────────────────────────────────────┘
```

Think in the terms of what you have experienced. What kind of things did you discuss? Why was it so important to come to a shared understanding of these things? How did you develop agreement? (Some may not have come to agreement in the allotted time.)

Transfer the sphere of reference from cars to group formation. Why do you think it's important for groups and group leaders to go through this process to develop a shared understanding of the small group they will form? Why would it be important for group members to share in this process even in a limited way?

By this time you probably recognize that reaching agreement on basic issues with a foursome is a challenge—let alone trying to mesh the expectations of eight to ten others. However, the "fun" and value you have experienced needs to be available in some measure to the larger group of members also. That's why it is important to discuss a covenant with the whole group early in the formation of the small group and to allow for some decision (potlucks or desserts) to be made by group members. This sense of decision-making gives group members a feeling of ownership which makes the group a higher investment for them than if they just come without participating.

EXPLORING AN IDEA

If you have coleaders in a small group, what kinds of things would be important for those leaders to come to agreement on before inviting others to join the group? If you are a solo leader, what expectations of yours are important to think through?

Trainer's Notes

Discuss these questions in groups of four. Some will want to go into greater detail here than others. Your concern is that they will cover the basics: purpose of the group, any distinctives, time and length of group, people mix, size of group, what will go on in the group, emphasis (i.e., prayer, personal study of Scripture, etc.). Ask for what your group members think is important and add in any they have missed. Be sure to ask for the reasons supporting their suggestions; it becomes a learning experience when you ask "why" an element is important when it is mentioned.

Why is it important for a person to know the purpose of a group before joining? What happens when you are part of a group where the purpose isn't clear?

Sometimes the fuzziness is in the language. For example, one group might state as a purpose "to grow in love." What, specifically, does this group do or not do? The broad purpose of growing together in love could include anything.

What happens when people in the group have different reasons for participating—one joining to meet lots of new people socially while another joins to share deeply about her growth in discipleship?

Trainer's Notes

You may want to add the importance of the following issues, either explaining what each means or giving illustrations showing the necessity of thinking through that issue:

- ▶ Commitment to regular attendance: what is excusable, what isn't, and why.
- ▶ Confidentiality.
- ▶ Baby-sitting—how it will be handled.
- ▶ Place of meeting—rotated or the same.
- ▶ Expectation that members will supply food, homes, etc.
- ▶ The kind of leadership you will supply—what is your responsibility and what isn't.

Open Vs. Closed Groups. An open group means anyone can join (visit) or leave the group at any point in the group duration. A closed group says you can count on the joining members to stay through the time period committed; no other members will be added during this time period once the group has officially formed. Small groups can remain open throughout their existence, or they can stay open for two or three sessions while persons are deciding if this group meets their purposes. After a specified time (two weeks) the group closes and members settle in for the period of commitment. Some groups close as soon as they are filled. What advantages and disadvantages do you see in each approach? When, and why, would you choose one over the other?

Some issues may not need to be thought through ahead of time for helping persons know if this is the small group for them. They may be discussed with the whole group the first time the small group is together. But remember: the larger the group, the longer the time period needed for group members to reach agreement.

The more realistically you think about your group, the more important some issues become. For example, food may not seem like a major issue; but when elaborate meals consume half of your group time, it can become detrimental. Or if you expected members to help with contacting people and they didn't plan on this, it is easy to feel resentful of the group members who aren't carrying their share of responsibility. The members need to know what is expected and need to share their expectations with the group as well. It is essential to share these positions and expectations before you get into the group and find your leadership team or your group divided on a major concern.

Just in talking together by foursomes, you may realize a kindred spirit in the others in your group and could work with them because many of your expectations mesh. Others may have found that people have very different ideas when they think of a "small group." Amos 3:3 states that unless two persons agree, they can't walk together. This is especially true in leading a group together. That doesn't mean that in every little detail you have to be "carbon copies"—but in main issues it is important to want the same things.

EXPERIENCING THE INSIGHT

Trainer's Notes

Refer group leaders to the Agreement Form and Checklist found on pages 33 and 35 as they work through the activities that follow.

To help in developing strong covenants, you have been provided a format which may aid you in writing up the "group" you expect to form. The Checklist is to help you think through any qualifying factors which can help prospective members in deciding whether yours is the small group for them. For instance, high cost for proposed ski trips may eliminate some persons from being in your group and they need to be aware of that at the beginning.

Paired Leaders. Pair up and discuss the issues outlined in the Agreement Form and the Checklist. Your partner should help you determine what you want to include and clarify all of your statements.

After 20–30 minutes pair up with a new partner. Read each other's covenants as a "prospective member" would read them, asking for clarification or making suggestions as needed.

Trainer's Notes

If your group leaders already have small groups or will soon be forming new groups, you might want to have group coleaders or leaders with similar group interests (e.g., those interested in forming young couples' groups) work together in the above exercise. Also, you might want to collect their covenants for publication and distribution to potential group members.

If groups have already been formed and your group leaders plan to contract with the whole group, use the Contracting at the First Meeting exercise. Should your situation be such that groups will together come up with their own covenants during the first or second session, use the Modeling exercise.

Contracting at the First Meeting. Come up with four or five key expectations for yourself as the group leader, each group member, and the group as a whole. These will serve as a framework for your sharing of your perspective with the group and prime the pump for members to share their expectations.

Modeling. This exercise should provide you with an understanding of how to come to agreement with a larger group. Choose a "leader" and form an impromptu group. Everyone else should roleplay new members of a small group and share how they really feel. See what items can be agreed on in forming this "new" group. The "leader" should ask questions such as the following:

▶ Why would you like to be a part of this group? What do you hope will happen?

▶ What do you think should be the purpose of our group? What do you think we should be or do?

▶ Is there anything in particular that you want to see emphasized or cultivated?

▶ What are your expectations of our relationships (both within the group and outside the group)?

▶ What is important for you to happen during group times? Not to happen during group times?

▶ How much time and energy can you give to this group?

After the "modeling" demonstration, discuss the exercise. Talk about how the "leader" handled the situations that arose. Discuss other ways these situations could have been handled. Remember: the responsibility of the leader is to help persons express strong feelings they have regarding the creation of a group to which they will commit. No leader is responsible to make everyone happy. A leader enables persons to see what is important to them and invites negotiation so that relationships and progress will not be hindered in the future because of hidden agendas. If you want to own a car, and you can't buy it on your own, you search for others who want something similar and are willing to commit to you and to agree on negotiations. This mutual commitment helps make the group "ours," not just the leader's, and breeds higher investment and responsibility.

A Word of Caution. If persons in your group are new Christians or new to small groups, beware of loading them with too extensive a covenant. Better to allow their commitments to grow with the group than to overwhelm them with too many expectations at the beginning.

Agreement Form

Type of Group (*circle one*)
      College
      Career/Single
      Mixed (singles & couples)
      Family (all ages or grade school and up?)
      Special Interest (Evangelism, camping, tennis)
      Young Marrieds (couples)
      Middle Marrieds (couples)
      Mature Marrieds (couples)
      Co-dependency Support—Chemical addiction
      Cancer Support (family)

Leaders: _____

Meeting Time:

Open Group (*How long open*):

Number Limit (*Including leaders*):

Purpose (*Why we will be together. Commitment expectations*):

Description (*What we will do*):

People This Group is Designed For:

Expectations (*What we expect of participants*):

Our Distinctives:

Checklist

Items to consider when writing up a contract, covenant, or agreement (*not all may apply to you*):

1. If you developed a contract last year, check your last year's copy—anything you want to *underscore?* State more strongly? Eliminate? Add now that you have "hindsight"?

2. Spell out "Commitment." What are you expecting when you use this word?

   ▶ To agree to be present at every meeting? To agree to be present at socials? To agree to attend a retreat?
   ▶ To agree to participate in monthly "prayer & share" dinners with another couple?
   ▶ To agree to share in opening their homes?
   ▶ To agree to share in providing food?
   ▶ To agree to share in teaching?
   ▶ To agree to share in calling others? To agree to pray regularly for group specifics on a daily calendar?
   ▶ To agree to other involvements?

3. What are your expectations of your "people mix"?

   ▶ Single, married? Number of each
   ▶ Age-level important?
   ▶ People who have never been in your group before?
   ▶ Number who are new to your church?
   ▶ Children at meetings? Children at socials?
   ▶ Age of children invited?
   ▶ Career/College age invited?
   ▶ People who do not already socialize together? People who do not know others on list?

4. What are your expectations of participants?

   ▶ They will supply their own baby-sitter? Or they will participate in co-op baby-sitting?

▶ They will go out to eat a lot and socialize once a month?
▶ They will be comfortable with expenses of entertainment?
▶ They will attend ski trips? Dramas? Musicals? Sports?
▶ They will become involved in developing a project?
▶ Everyone in the group will participate verbally?
▶ They will each purchase a book?
▶ They will be open to leading a group themselves next year?

5. What are the distinctives of your group?

▶ All must be tennis players? Experienced? Novice?
▶ Participants must have teenagers in the home?
▶ Emphasis on community involvement?
▶ Emphasis on 30-minute prayer time each meeting?
▶ Involvement in missions?
▶ High accountability with meeting/calling weekly one other person from the group?
▶ Involvement in projects such as:

> sponsoring a family?
> surveying the community?
> winning a neighbor to Christ?
> spending time weekly with your teenager?
> once a month serve meals to homeless?
> regular exercise?

Pick out only the things that are priorities to you. Word your contract as briefly as possible. Make your priorities stand out. Do you want members to have a copy of their contract?

During your first or second meeting, discuss this contract and allow those who don't feel comfortable to opt out and go to another group. Where possible, reform this contract to fit the expectations of leader and members and then invite each to commit to this until the group agrees to change it or until the contractual period is over. This commitment gives a sense of security as each realizes what is required and commits him/herself to following through on agreed upon items.

This kind of foundation creates a strong, secure group.

In the course of leaders writing down what is important to them, you may also want to supply sample copies of agreements already written.

Two things are extremely important as you write an agreement: *priority* and *clarity.*

Write simply so there isn't a lot of vague language to go through. For example, instead of "We want to love each other and be better Christians," write what that means in your expectations. Perhaps it means, "We will make contact with another couple in our group each week to follow up on prayer requests."

Second, what is important to you needs to stand out. "Persons committing to this group agree to become involved in the discussion in a vital way and not sit back and watch."

For Your Information. Below are included the covenant dynamics as identified by Louis H. Evans, Jr. in his book, *Creative Love* (Revell, 1977). Also below is the Serendipity Covenant required of all who would participate in the Serendipity Bible studies program.

Covenants of Creative Love

1. **The Covenant of Affirmation** (unconditional love, agape love) There is nothing you have done or will do that will make me stop loving you. I may not agree with your actions, but I will love you as a person and do all I can to hold you up in God's affirming love.

2. **The Covenant of Availability** Anything I have—time, energy, insight, possessions—are all at your disposal if you need them. I give these to you in a priority of covenant over non-covenant demands. As part of this availability I pledge regularity of time, whether in prayer or in agreed upon meeting time.

3. **The Covenant of Prayer** I covenant to pray for you in some regular fashion, believing that our caring Father

desires His children to pray for one another and ask Him for the blessings they need.

4. **The Covenant of Openness** I promise to strive to become a more open person, disclosing my feelings, my struggles, my joys, and my hurts to you as well as I am able. The degree to which I do so implies that I cannot make it without you, that I trust you with my needs and that I need you. This is to affirm your worth to me as a person. In other words, I need you!

5. **The Covenant of Sensitivity** Even as I desire to be known and understood by you, I covenant to be sensitive to you and to your needs to the best of my ability. I will try to hear you, see you, and feel where you are to draw you out of the pit of discouragement or withdrawal.

6. **The Covenant of Honesty** I will try to "mirror back" to you what I am hearing you say and feel. If this means risking pain for either of us I will trust our relationship enough to take that risk, realizing it is in "speaking the truth in love, that we grow up in every way into Christ who is the Head." I will try to express this honesty, to "meter it," according to what I perceive the circumstances to be.

7. **The Covenant of Confidentiality** I consider that the gifts God has given me for the common good should be liberated for your benefit. If I should discover areas of my life that are under bondage, "hung up" or truncated by my own misdoings or by the scars inflicted by others, I will seek Christ's liberating power through my covenant partners so that I might give to you more of myself. I am accountable to you to "become what God has designed me to be in His loving creation."

The Serendipity Covenant

1. **Attendance:** Priority is given to the group meetings. Except in cases of emergency, you will be present and on time.

2. **Participation:** The purpose of the first 6 sessions is to get acquainted and build up a sense of oneness, or "koinonia," in your group. This is accomplished by letting each group member "tell his or her spiritual story" to the group. To be in a group, you must be willing to let the group hear "your story."

3. **Confidentiality:** Anything that is shared in the group is kept in strict confidence. This is not a therapy group, but information will be shared from time to time that should not be repeated outside the group.

4. **Accountability:** The group is for people who know they are weak and need the help of others to overcome temptation, spiritual depression, and chronic weakness. In asking to be in a group, you are admitting you need support . . . and that you are willing to support others in the same condition. To be in a group, you are giving others permission to call on you for spiritual help — even at three o'clock in the morning — and you are asking for the same permission from others.

5. **Evangelism:** The group is willing and ready at any time to adopt new people who need the support and correction of your group. In forming a group, you also agree to "keep an empty chair" for anyone who needs your help and is willing to agree to these minimum disciplines.

EQUIPPING SESSION 3

POINT OF CONTACT
How to Build
a Small Group

. . . .

TARGET
By the end of this session you will:

▶ Become aware of various types of needs present in a small group.
▶ Recognize signs of these needs.
▶ Want to help group members have those needs met.
▶ Learn how to create a climate of trust.
▶ Learn how to utilize skills to build a group.
▶ Become aware of your own needs and how they affect the role of leadership.
▶ Participate in needs assessment and skill development.

MATERIALS NEEDED
Moveable chairs
Overhead projector

Blank transparencies, chalkboard, or newsprint for recording responses
Envelope with slips of nonverbal expression

IDENTIFYING THE ISSUE

Sift through your awareness and write down on a piece of paper all the reasons that prompted you to come to this session. Look for reasons behind the first answers that come to mind. For instance, "I had to come because 'so-and-so' asked me" may really be "I want 'so-and-so' to like me so I did what she asked." See how aware you are of the "real" agenda that brought you here. After a few moments share for one minute with another person what you became aware of.

What reasons are you aware of as to why persons join a group? List these.

Trainer's Notes

You might want to suggest the following reasons for joining a group: want to work toward group's goals, attracted to other members or leader, want personal needs met, need a sense of belonging, want friends and a place to socialize.

When you meet with your group members all these desires may be present. It's possible that people come expecting results in each of these areas. As leader you also come with an agenda of what you would like to see accomplished as well as how you would like your group to see you as a leader.

An apt picture that describes all that goes on in a small group setting would be that of a three-ring circus. Sometimes we focus on one ring more than another or we are distracted by activity in one ring and miss what takes place in another, but always there is something of interest going on in each of the three rings. As leader you act as ringmaster, calling attention to major events of emphasis so participants won't miss out. The ringmaster is aware of what is happening in all three spheres and knows which to accent when. Growth in leadership skills allows you to do just that.

Trainer's Notes

To facilitate the following discussion, display (on newsprint or overhead transparency) the three basic agendas.

Group researchers advise us that there are three basic agendas facing every small group.

1. Individual needs that must be met. For example, I need people to like me as a person; I need to feel I am worthwhile.

2. The group task must be accomplished. In a committee type group this means completing the agenda. In other groups this agenda might be "we had a Bible study," or "we got to know each other in a personal way." Without a task or purpose, groups don't feel there is a reason to exist.

3. The maintaining of group relationships. What happens to people as the task is being accomplished? How do they feel about each other and how are they learning to deal with each other?

As you look at these three, which do you think the ringmaster would give heavier emphasis to in a beginning group?

Because the need of greatest awareness to a person is an individual one, the leader must begin by acting in awareness of individual needs such as security and care and esteem.

Committees often begin with task—what is important to the leader—and find that persons will not take responsibility or will even react by withholding, questioning, judging, etc. the task because of personal threat or doubt. "If I don't make a critical statement, they will think I'm not intelligent"; or "If I disagree with this idea, they may not want me on this committee so I will just sit back and let it happen until I know more about this committee." An experienced leader knows that a group cannot survive on meeting personal needs alone and so moves quickly into helping persons learn how to work together and to feel good about who they are as members of a group. So begin with #1, move quickly into #3, and introduce #2 so persons recognize a balance.

You probably learned how to play tic-tac-toe as a child. There is now a more complicated, multidimensional version in which straights can be made horizontally, diagonally, and in depth. In a similar way, each of the three basic agendas become complicated by three dynamics which operate at the same time. The three dynamics that affect a group are:

▶ Power and influence.
▶ Acceptance and belonging.
▶ Accomplishment.

Group members need all three for growth. While a person may not be aware of his or her actions or words being prompted by one of these particular dynamics, one of these is behind each person's response. A good leader works at providing a sense of all of these. Activities and comments in the materials are designed to give members a sense of one or more of these. They are "Hidden Persuaders" that help a person to feel known, valued, and ready to grow.

EXPERIENCING THE INSIGHT
Try out this idea by recognizing the hidden persuader in each of the below. In clusters of three talk over whether the item speaks to the dynamic of *power and influence, acceptance and belonging,* or *accomplishment,* and whether the item would build or undermine each of these dynamics.

44

1. Group rituals such as seating arrangements and the way the session *always* begins.
2. "We want to hear from each of you as to how you feel about this."
3. Inside jokes known only to the group.
4. "Stan, why don't you summarize what we've decided."
5. "How many agree with Debbie's idea?"
6. "In your groups of four, come up with a way you want to celebrate and then do it."
7. Inviting members to sign up to provide refreshments.
8. "What's one thing you've learned and will put into practice as a result of this study?"
9. "Let's clarify what we said we want to see happen at each of our group times. And if this isn't your understanding, let us know."
10. Introductions by giving name and title you are known by (e.g., Program Researcher, Mother, Doctor, Boss, etc.).

Trainer's Notes

You might suggest the following answers to above exercise if the group is stumped:

1. belonging, building
2. belonging and power, building
3. belonging, building
4. accomplishment, building
5. power, undermining
6. power, building
7. belonging, building
8. accomplishment, building
9. power and accomplishment and belonging, building
10. acceptance and power, questionable

The Johari Window. Most members of your group will not be aware of this process consciously. They do come, however, with an awareness of many of the things they want from a group. Helping the whole group become aware of these expectations is a goal of the leader. Sometimes a leader also must help an individual become aware of personal reasons for behavior. Becoming "aware" is the first step in doing something about a need. For instance, some people have a tremendous need to be right. These folks may come across as argumentative or dogmatic in their statements and be repulsed by the rest of the group. What the individual may know is that "people usually don't like me and what I say." Or the person may claim, "I am who I am and if people don't like what I say, that's their problem." But the need to be right in order to be OK is hidden from them.

The Johari Window (pronounced as though combining Joe and Harry) was developed by Joseph Luft and Harrington V. Ingham as a model to show awareness in interpersonal relations. It is made up of four quadrants.

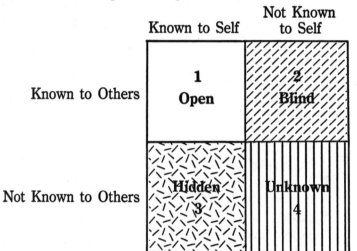

Quadrant 1 represents what is *known* by the self and by others in the areas of behavior, feelings, and motivations. "I always shake hands or formally present myself when I am introduced to someone."

Quadrant 2 is called the *blind* area because the person is blind to the behaviors, feelings, and motivations which others may see. "I may feel I am a friendly person while others see me as reserved and private, using the formal to keep my distance."

Quadrant 3 is the *hidden* area of my life which I know but others don't. "I remember being betrayed by a relationship in the past where I trusted a friend."

Quadrant 4 is called *unknown* because neither the person nor those in the group know this part of the individual. It is undiscovered.

The lines illustrating the size of these quadrants move as the group interacts over time. Draw lines showing the size of the quadrants as they represent the "Knowing" that is present in your group at this stage.

Explore with your cluster some implications of this awareness model.

	Known to Self	Not Known to Self
Known to Others	**1** **Open**	**2** **Blind**
Not Known to Others	**Hidden** **3**	**Unknown** **4**

Trainer's Notes

Encourage group leaders to use the following questions to facilitate their discussions of the Johari Window.

1. Our goal is to help persons move in the direction of appropriate self-disclosure. When a person shares too much too soon, what happens to that person? To others in the group?

47

2. When a person is not given opportunity to share more than content answers, what happens?

3. A change that takes place in any one quadrant will affect all the other quadrants. Why?

4. It requires energy to deny, block out, or hide behavior that is revealed in group interaction. "I did not withdraw from the group when Bill said women weren't conscious of overall issues." Why might a person want to deny revealed behavior?

5. Trust seems to help increase awareness, and people tend to value a group that has greater awareness. True or false? Why?

6. The smaller quadrant 1 is, the poorer the quality of communication in the group. Why is this true? What is an example of this?

7. What is an insight into your small group that has occurred as you have discussed these ideas with your cluster? Share it with your cluster to increase quadrant 1 in your cluster.

(Johari ideas taken from *Group Processes*, 3rd edition, by Joseph Luft, Mayfield Publishing Company, 1984.)

Body Language. Sometimes the "hidden informers" about what a person is really saying come through nonverbal signs.

Learning to read what a person's nonverbal cues are telling you is an art.

Body language can mean many different things. Therefore it is *always* helpful to check with the individual about the meaning. Give feedback by describing the action observed and then inquiring as to its meaning. For example, "I noticed that you moved your chair away from the circle after you shared that you couldn't work on the project with us. Were you making a statement by doing that?" or "Does this mean that something is going on inside you?" If you identify a possible cause, always state it tentatively. "Does this mean that you are . . . ?" But remember: give the person a chance to agree or disagree with your statement. Do not play amateur psychologist. You are trying to help people reveal who they really are and what they really feel so you can build trust in the group and a sense of cohesion with persons you know.

Persons tend to communicate more openly through nonverbal cues. Those who have studied this phenomenon suggest that the lower lip is the clearest indicator of emotion. It is the most difficult part of the body to mask when an emotion is felt.

If a person seems uninvolved verbally, check the individual's nonverbal signs. Do they suggest that the person really is involved and tracking with the group, but just not communicating with words?

When a person makes a statement do the nonverbal signs match or do they betray something else? "We all said 'yes' to spending a day together to get acquainted, but I picked up some signals that made me wonder if you all felt OK about our decision. Maybe we should talk about it some more. What do you think?" Or "Mark, I sense you feel stronger about this than maybe the rest of us do—would you care to share further?" Such observations may open to your group unique opportunities to value differences, to maintain a climate of accepting honesty, or to minister to a misunderstanding or deep feeling.

EXPERIENCING THE INSIGHT

Trainer's Notes

Hand out envelopes with slips of paper which state the following:

▶ Paper 1—Picture yourself in a small group where someone has just verbally attacked a conviction of yours. How do you communicate defensiveness nonverbally in your facial expression?

▶ Paper 2—In a small group you are afraid you are going to be asked to share about an area where you really don't want to reveal your thoughts because you may be judged. How do you communicate your fear in your facial expression?

▶ Paper 3—In your small group you feel like people are going off on a tangent, and you are nervous that the group isn't going to accomplish what you hoped for. How do you communicate your anxiety in your facial expression?

Facial expression, especially eye contact, or the lack of it, can reveal what a person is feeling or thinking. In your clusters of three, have each person draw from the envelope a slip of paper on which is written a response for you to portray to the others using facial expression only. Let the other two respond to you with what they read in your expression. How would you minister care to this individual?

Discuss the following list of "hidden informers." What could each of these "hidden informers" suggest?

▶ A tapping pencil or foot could say:

▶ Rubbing a nose, clasping and unclasping of hands, constant clearing of throat could signify:

▶ A clenched fist could indicate:

▶ A palm to chest could mean:

Give at least two meanings that the following could indicate.

Sitting slumped

Trying to blend into chair

Placing hands on hips

Fading voice

Rapid rate of speech

Saying nothing

Sitting on the outskirts of a circle

Leaning forward

Monopolizing the conversation

Sudden straightening

Increasing volume

Folding arms over chest

Sitting behind another person rather than in the front row

EXPLORING AN IDEA

Sensitizing yourself to what people are communicating is the first step in creating a climate where growth can take place. Some people are naturally aware of these signs and others need to work at cultivating receptivity to what a person is saying.

Some people adopt a conversation style that says straight out what they are thinking and feeling. Others have grown up with a style that feels it is impolite to say directly what you are thinking and feeling, so they hint. Here's an example: "Well, I don't know if I should take on that responsibility." "Then you don't want to head up this event?" "Well, I didn't say that." "So you will take the lead on this?" "Well, if you folks really think I can do it and want me in that position?" "Of course, we want you—you're the best at this kind of thing." "Oh, I am not: others do just as well in organizing." And on and on it goes.

Some personality types are exact in their responses and some abhor the routine of exactness.

"So how many were at the meeting?"
"Oh, around 12 or so."
"You had 12 present?"
"Give or take a few."
"Well, which was it? Give or take?"
"I don't know. It was somewhere in the neighborhood of 10 or 12. I really didn't count them. It wasn't important."
"It *is* important: we need to know *exactly*, for the record. Why can't you just say 11 persons were there. That's what I'll put down or we'll be here all night on this."

Then there are differences between those who are basically task-oriented, bent on achieving the goal so persons (including themselves) will feel good about the group, and those who seem satisfied to just enjoy the people, whether they *go* anywhere or not.

"All right, let's press on or we'll never get through this chapter."

"But I want to hear from Esther. She was about to give us her view on commitment. I think it's important to hear from everyone."

"Well, theoretically it is, but if we are to be ready for chapter 3 next time, we can't have everyone share on every verse."

"What does it matter if we get to verse 22. We're learning some important things about people's view of commitment. The more we know each other the better this group will be."

Of course, no one deliberately sets out to thwart and exasperate those who are different. When we see another person as bothersome or antagonistic because of some difference, we butt heads and don't build cohesion. How can you build a climate of understanding and trust? What can you do to construct this? How can you let others know who these persons are?

The more a person reveals, the greater you will identify with him or her. An unknown individual is often misinterpreted and eyed with suspicion. Questions that allow others to share with you what has been their past experiences will help you find points of contact. Sharing feelings, as well as facts, is extremely important if you want to know someone and come to trust him. Capitalizing on every opportunity that gives people a chance to tell who they are builds a sense of understanding and commitment.

EXPERIENCING THE INSIGHT
Examine the sharing questions below. How do you feel about each? Why? What principles can you create for good sharing questions that build a sense of trust?

53

Sharing Questions

1. Tell us about your childhood.
2. What do you know about the Pharisees?
3. What was your most embarrassing moment?
4. When is a time when God became very real to you?
5. What relationship has made a significant impact on who you are as a Christian today?
6. What kind of things do you worry about?
7. Share three adjectives that describe you from your viewpoint.
8. What three qualities would the person closest to you say you possess?
9. What is your favorite time of the day and why?
10. Tell your three strongest points. Tell your three weakest points.
11. What is a word that describes God to you and why do you choose that word?
12. What car are you most like?

Draw principles from the above questions. For example: "Questions need to be limited by some boundaries (determined by the purpose) rather than so broad the respondent is unsure of how to answer.

Trainer's Notes

Share the following analysis of the previous sharing questions to guide the group leaders' discussion:

1. Vague—too broad.
2. Information based—may feel ignorant or proud of knowledge. Not a sharing question—don't get to know person.
3. Could be hard to share. Or could become a "can you top this situation."
4. Good, assuming all Christians.
5. Good, not limited—can choose level of importance. Person will probably include meaning of choice in answering.

6. Threat to new group. Since the word "most" isn't included, persons may be willing to share on a generic level, but then you don't really get to know them.
7. OK. Two might be better time-wise. Personal evaluation is hard for some, but in this question they can choose the level of risk.
8. OK. Free to choose level of risk and affirming.
9. OK. Includes all and asks for meaning.
10. Threatening. Three could be quite hard for some.
11. Good. One word so uncomplicated. Asks for meaning.
12. Assumes knowledge of cars. Could be used if this knowledge present. Should be followed by, "Why did you choose this one?"

Another way to build trust and a sense of belonging is to be emotionally supportive to a person's response. Periodic "Um's" assure a person that you are listening.

Giving words of specific commendation build self-esteem. "I thought you handled that question very tactfully" rather than "You did a good job."

Sharing words of relationship supports another. "You are an encourager to me by the way in which you respond enthusiastically."

God is the great Encourager. Though aware of our needs, He gently helps us become aware and then supports us as we pursue growth. Of what need has He made you aware as you have explored this subject?

Paul writing to the Philippians assures them in the material realm that God "will meet all your needs according to his glorious riches in Christ Jesus" (4:19). God's power and wisdom give Him the balance needed to help you grow. Close by telling your Father of the need of which you have become aware. Pray in pairs.

EQUIPPING SESSION 4

IT PAYS TO
READ THE DIRECTIONS
How to Lead a Good
Small Group Session

. . . .

TARGET

By the end of this session you will:

▶ Know the purposes behind the design of a lesson.
▶ Learn how to utilize written materials to achieve those purposes.
▶ Be motivated to lead group sessions that promote change.
▶ Select one insight to incorporate into your own small group session.
▶ Demonstrate skill in putting the above into practice.

MATERIALS NEEDED

Moveable chairs
Overhead projector
Blank transparencies, chalkboard, or newsprint for recording
   responses

Visual display of *Hook, Book, Look,* and *Took.*
Newsprint and markers

IDENTIFYING THE ISSUE
What would you say is the purpose of a blueprint? What is the benefit of a handbook? Why use a map? Why read directions printed on the box? What is the purpose of small group curriculum materials?

Some persons stick closely to the steps described in the directions when they work on installing a household item. Others refer to the directions for overall ideas and to supplement their lack of insight. Few, unless they have had much previous experience, ignore the provided insights that lead to a successful completion of their project. They realize that the blueprint reflects the overall design of the developer.

Well-designed small group materials develop good small groups. They are constructed to help persons grasp ideas. They are written with an awareness of the feelings and values held by persons in a group and carefully build toward motivating those persons to act on those attitudes and values. The content seeks to build a bridge to the life experiences of the people in your group. And the action called for to implement ideas helps members take steps in the direction of obeying the truth of Scripture and experiencing the satisfaction of moving in the direction of growth.

For the desired product to function as promised by the manufacturer, it is imperative to understand and carry out the basic plan of the designer. As a group leader, you get to go behind the scenes and discover what goes into developing materials that produce the results you desire. What makes the process interesting is that you as leader become part of the team as you *adapt* and *tailor-fit* each lesson to your group; much like a "tailor-made suit" is shaped to the contours of the individual, but the overall design is the same for everyone.

EXPLORING AN IDEA

If your major purpose was simply the delivery of information, you would have a far easier time. You could tell group members the information and then devise ways to have them give it back to you to test for grasp of facts. Machines that reveal informative materials could be used instead of persons as leaders.

But small groups focus in a major way on what is happening to people. Only a personal guide can respond to people and cultivate attitudes that lead to the application of knowledge.

The lesson content then should not absorb the whole evening. It is primarily a springboard to promote discussion among persons for understanding and applying to life. It provides opportunity to explore biblical principles in light of living. This means:

▶ The lesson must not be centered around a lecture.
▶ The lesson must not be dominated by the group leader.
▶ The leader is not an "answer man or woman."
▶ The content is a vital part of the lesson, forming the heart of the discussion.
▶ The lesson must be tailored to your particular group.
▶ It is important to stay with the curriculum rather than digressing to another topic, if you want to build continuity and structure for actual growth.

Trainer's Notes

Before continuing with the discussion, refer group leaders to the Small Group Session and Leader's Guide found on pages 75-79.

What's the Pattern? What major sections do you find in the Small Group Session provided for your examination?

The section called *Session Objectives* in the Leader's Guide is like the completed picture on the box of a jigsaw puzzle. It tells you what the group will be when all the pieces of the session have been inserted.

The three major sections of the session are: *Getting Acquainted, Gaining Insight,* and *Growing By Doing.* These sections grow out of each other and build on what has gone before. They incorporate the following four steps common to most curriculum lesson plans: *Hook, Book, Look,* and *Took.*

```
─────────────── Trainer's Notes ───────────────
Display a list of these four steps as you continue the
discussion.
```

Getting Acquainted (Hook). What are the most important minutes in a TV program? It is generally assumed that if you aren't "hooked" in the first 5 minutes of a program, you will probably switch channels. Think about the advertising pieces you receive in your home. What are some of the "hooks" on the outside of the envelopes to get you to look inside?

The first step is motivation. You cannot assume that people come to small groups motivated to grow and respond. Some may come preoccupied or tired or not even thinking about the subject to be explored. Knowing people and knowing where your group is coming from helps you create some sparks of interest as you bridge from what they have experienced to what they will experience in the group.

Getting acquainted or reacquainted with the persons in the group is also required for motivation. The more members bond and feel at ease with others, the more open they are to explore new ideas and to incorporate new insights into what they already do. Techniques used in the *Getting Acquainted* section include gaming, discussion questions, survey, testing, interviews, case studies, and cartoons.

The purpose of *Getting Acquainted* is to get group members

interested in exploring a subject with persons they know and like and responding as individuals who have something to contribute. Take enough time to arouse interest, but don't spend the bulk of your time on this area. It is only a means to an end.

Look at Small Group Session and discuss with another group leader how "getting acquainted" is accomplished in this session. How do the suggested ideas motivate? Do they show a lack? Arouse a question? Stimulate interest? Reveal knowledge or convictions?

Which of the suggested ideas in the *Getting Acquainted* section of the Leader's Guide would you likely choose and why? Would you use it as is or adapt it to fit your group in some particular way?

Gaining Insight (Book). When motivated to explore an idea, you want group members to see how what God has to say about the subject relates to their questions and concerns. This is accomplished in the section called *Gaining Insight.* It is important that group members understand not only the issues they have identified but also understand the principles God has supplied for our living as believers. Sometimes this means enlarging our concept of who He is. Sometimes it means understanding the guidelines which He has developed. Sometimes it means learning from biblical examples of persons who lived by or didn't live by the principles He has given.

With your partner, take five minutes to circle all the insights you can find in the Small Group Session and Leader's Guide. Try to identify the direction of each insight—Is it knowledge about God, a principle to live by, or an example showing how to live a principle?

The more a leader can guide group members into discovering insights for themselves, the more these truths will become a part of them and the more interest members will have. Telling doesn't do it. That's why discussion questions are used extensively in the Bible study. Remember: you must get group members into the Word themselves! What did you spot in this section that demonstrates this principle? How did group members get involved in discovery learning?

This kind of search and discover learning takes time as group members go through the process. But good small groups are more than "content stuffers." The process of grasping content is as important as the content itself if lives are to be changed by it.

Growing By Doing (Look and Took). These two steps are so closely related that they are often linked together. The *Look* step is a bridge from the understanding of the principle to the life of the person. *Look* asks for all the ways a principle could affect the life of the person who understands it.

Consider the mathematical principle: $2 + 2 = 4$. What are some areas of your life that are affected because you *know* and *understand* this principle? If you didn't understand this principle, you'd probably have problems making change at the grocery, balancing your checkbook, or making reservations for dinner. You probably learned to write your name so long ago that it is hard to remember how this impacted your life. But think back to all the possibilities that opened to you when those formerly meaningless letter symbols of vowels and consonants were suddenly realized as representing you. Knowing this means that you can now identify your materials, place ownership on your papers, respond to written instructions addressed to you, spot mail addressed to you, sign checks, and many other things.

The *Look* section helps a principle make sense in your life. It is usually grasped by asking people to think through aspects of their lives which could be affected by knowing this. For example, you might ask group members how a principle might impact their schedules, relationships, actions, attitudes, communication, spending money, dealing with the past, present, or future, or handling a situation. As a group leader, you can prime the pump with illustrations and examples—but group members need to think of their own issues if they are to relate a principle to their lives.

Again, go back to the Small Group Session and Leader's Guide and under *Growing By Doing* underline something that is designed to help group members take a *look* at their lives in relation to a principle.

Trainer's Notes

Briefly recap the steps for your group leaders.

▶ *Hook* is to motivate (10–15 minutes).

▶ *Book* is to discover and understand biblical principles (15–25 minutes).

▶ *Look* is to hold those principles up against our lives to discover as many practical ways as possible where they affect our lives (15–25 minutes).

Took. After discovering *how* to respond and *where* they could respond in their lives, will group members do it? Probably not. Most know (and are even convinced) of the truth of God's Word. They are aware of areas of their lives which would be affected if they put the Truth into practice. What causes persons to actually follow through in doing just that—putting Truth into practice in one area of their lives?

Look at the following Scripture passages and identify in the margin what can happen as a result of knowing and understanding the Word of God (the *Took*). Circle each *Took* for which you can name at least one way in which you have experienced it in your own life.

[16]All Scripture is God-breathed and is useful for teaching, rebuking, correcting and training in righteousness, [17]so that the man of God may be thoroughly equipped for every good work.

2 Timothy 3:16-17

[1]Blessed is the man who does not walk in the counsel of the wicked or stand in the way of sinners or sit in the seat of mockers. [2]But his delight is in the law of the LORD, and on His law he meditates day and night. [3]He is like a tree planted by streams of water, which yields its fruit in season and whose leaf does not wither. Whatever he does prospers.

Psalm 1:1-3

[12]In fact, though by this time you ought to be teachers, you need someone to teach you the elementary truths of God's word all over again. You need milk, not solid food! [13]Anyone who lives on milk, being still an infant, is not acquainted with the teaching about righteousness. [14]But solid food is for the mature, who by constant use have trained themselves to distinguish good from evil.

Hebrews 5:12-14

[99]I have more insight than all my teachers, for I meditate on Your statutes. [100]I have more understanding than the elders, for I obey Your precepts. [101]I have kept my feet from every evil path so that I might obey Your word. [102]I have not departed from Your laws, for You Yourself have taught me. [103]How sweet are our words to my taste, sweeter than honey to my mouth!

Psalm 119:99-103

What is one thing you see in these passages that comes as a *Took* for those who put the content of Scripture into practice?

Here is another illustration of *Took:* You attend a fair on ecology and conservation. One booth offers you a free energy conservation kit with items to install to save energy elements. You agree with this goal and see yourself as a caretaker of the earth. You realize you are responsible for preserving the earth for generations to come, some of whom you know personally as children or grandchildren. What will guarantee your going home and installing the energy-saving equipment?

What will encourage your doing it? You might want to consider the following: accountability, reminders, someone doing it with you, immediate application, picking one specific act and setting aside a definite time to do it in your schedule, or identifying one specific person who will be a part of your carrying out what you have decided to do. All of these actions enable us to do what we know.

Actually, being in a group is an excellent motivation as others who surround you also work at doing what they know. How else do you see a group setting as an asset for doing the Truth?

Sometimes love for and responsibility to others helps us follow through. Groups who give each other the right to hold one another accountable promote change. Actually doing what is known right in the setting of the group increases the likelihood of an individual doing the same thing on his or her own. For example, a group that affirms one another is probably going to do that when apart.

Took cannot be forced, only enabled. In a group this is done by helping members select a specific way to apply truth and, whenever possible, actually doing it right then in the group. The purpose has been aborted if this living of truth does not take place. God is interested in our doing something about what we know. This means actual application in one specific way.

As you identified life application areas in the *Look* portion (*Growing By Doing*) of the Small Group Session, how could you help your group move in the direction of actually acting on what is known? With your partner, come up with one way you could do this, other than what is listed under *Growing By Doing*. This is not easy, but it is vital. After 8–10 minutes share suggestions so all benefit from seeing many ways to move into this important last step.

This is the key to a growing group: where people actually become responsive to God's truth in their lives. The Wrigley Company is not content to have you sing their jingle or recognize their product—they want you to chew their gum!

IDENTIFYING THE ISSUE

--- **Trainer's Notes** ---

This final section will help your group leaders put the principles they have learned into practice. Allow at least 20 minutes for groups to work on these ideas. Then ask two groups to join and report to each other the results of their thinking in 5–7 minutes.

Find two or three other leaders with whom you feel comfortable. Move to a section of the room where your group can work. Choose one of the following projects for your group to work on.

Our small group wants to:

Project #1—Become vegetarian in our eating habits.
Project #2—Pray for one another as prayer partners during the week.
Project #3—Get involved in some form of exercise.
Project #4—Respond to the plight of AIDS victims.
Project #5—Buy the right kind of insurance plan.

In the space provided, write next to *Hook, Book* (content of any kind), *Look,* and *Took* .one way you would accomplish each of these steps to cause your group members to complete the selected project. For example: How could you motivate for this cause (*Hook*)? How could you give them content on this cause (*Book*)? How could it affect their lives (*Look*)? What do you want them to do about it (*Took*)?

Hook—

Book—

Look—

Took—

Think through the following responses:

▶ Where have you been strongest, weakest in your small group lesson?

▶ What new insight have you gained or what known idea has been reinforced in this behind-the-scenes exploration of the written material?

▶ What is one step you will take in your next small group session as a result of this insight? Share that with one other person who is here.

Close by praying for implementation of the shared idea.

SMALL GROUP STUDENT SESSION

Choices

GroupSpeak: *"Different people desire different things from a group. In a way, that was a shock to me because I knew what I wanted to get out of our group, and I assumed that everyone else wanted that, too. But that didn't turn out to be true. People choose to be in a group for different reasons."*

You Have a Choice!

Strawberry Creme?	Vanilla?	Cherry?
Chocolate Ripple?	Butter Brickle?	Peach?
Small?	Medium?	Large?
Ice Milk?	Yogurt?	Premium?

Our world knows the value of having a choice. Baskin Robbins created and built an empire on making available 31 flavors from which to choose. We choose the brand of coffee we drink and whether we want our cereal honey-sweetened, in circles, flakes, or nuggets. Most of us probably selected the car we drive on the basis of economy, color, model, accessories available, usefulness to your purposes.

Choices are a fun part of life. We enjoy the freedom of selection put under our control. Having a choice means we don't have to accept what we receive. It gives us a feeling of value as well as a sense of responsibility. While we may "get what we ask for," we must also live with the choices we make.

Let's examine the choices involved in a small group as we meet together for the first time. We'll learn who we are in terms of our choices. We'll focus on what it means to be "chosen" and rejoice over God's choices. Finally, we'll look at what responsibilities go along with choices.

GETTING ACQUAINTED

Birds of a Feather
After your **Group Leader** designates three distinct areas of the room as **A, B,** and **C,** indicate your choice among the three options by moving to the appropriate area that represents your preference.

Do you prefer	A	B	C
a vacation at the	beach	mountains	desert/other

Where specifically do you like to go?

studying	Gospels	Epistles	Psalms

What's a favorite book/section?

living in the	city	suburbs	rural area

What do you like about your choice?

watching	comedy	drama	science fiction

Why did you make this choice?

eating food that is	salty	sweet	sour

And your favorite is?

relaxing by	reading a book	exercising	taking a nap

Why did you choose this?

sitting in church   at the back   in the middle at the front

Why?

_____

Did you notice some of the same people kept showing up in your group? Find someone who made some of the same selections as yourself and affirm him or her for making such wise choices!

GAINING INSIGHT

Understanding Choices
Life is filled with choices. List some choices you've made today.

Choices made this morning: Choices made this afternoon:

_____   _____

_____   _____

_____   _____

_____   _____

_____   _____

Turn to your neighbor and share at least five choices you've made today.

Choices are important for involvement in a small group. Our choices reveal who we are. Being in a small group community means we will be making choices based on our expectations and desires. We have chosen to be obedient to Jesus who has commanded us to relate to one another as His body, the church. He has called us to be the church, not just go to church. And becoming a part of a small group is one of the best ways to get involved in fulfilling that calling.

You have chosen to place yourself in a situation where it is highly probable that you will be called upon to grow and to join with others in putting the Word of God into practice.

Scripture Study

Let's examine what the Bible has to say about the formation of Jesus' small group—a group of 12 whose lives would be revolutionized by being together with Him as their leader. Read the following Scripture passage, noting those whom Jesus chose to become a part of His group.

³⁵The next day John was there again with two of his disciples. ³⁶When he saw Jesus passing by, he said, "Look, the Lamb of God!"

³⁷When the two disciples heard him say this, they followed Jesus. ³⁸Turning around, Jesus saw them following and asked, "What do you want?"

They said, "Rabbi" (which means Teacher), "where are You staying?"

³⁹"Come," He replied, "and you will see."

So they went and saw where He was staying, and spent that day with Him. It was about the tenth hour.

⁴⁰Andrew, Simon Peter's brother, was one of the two who heard what John had said and who had followed Jesus. ⁴¹The first thing Andrew did was to find his brother Simon and tell him, "We have found the Messiah" (that is, the Christ). ⁴²And he brought him to Jesus.

Jesus looked at him and said, "You are Simon son of John. You will be called Cephas" (which, when translated, is Peter).

⁴³The next day Jesus decided to leave for Galilee. Finding Philip, He said to him, "Follow Me."

⁴⁴Philip, like Andrew and Peter, was from the town of Bethsaida. ⁴⁵Philip found Nathanael and told him, "We have found the one Moses wrote about in the Law, and about

71

whom the prophets also wrote—Jesus of Nazareth, the son of Joseph."

⁴⁶"Nazareth! Can anything good come from there?" Nathanael asked.

"Come and see," said Philip.

⁴⁷When Jesus saw Nathanael approaching, He said to him, "Here is a true Israelite, in whom there is nothing false."

⁴⁸"How do You know me?" Nathanael asked.

Jesus answered, "I saw you while you were still under the fig tree before Philip called you."

⁴⁹Then Nathanael declared, "Rabbi, You are the Son of God; You are the King of Israel."

⁵⁰Jesus said, "You believe because I told you I saw you under the fig tree. You shall see greater things than that." ⁵¹He then added, "I tell you the truth, you shall see heaven open, and the angels of God ascending and descending on the Son of Man."

John 1:35-51

What choices did Jesus' followers make in this passage?

In what ways could the disciples' choices affect the rest of their lives?

It's energizing to be a chooser—to realize that the choices you make to pursue a relationship can impact the rest of your life. There is power in choosing—there is also responsibility.

In Jesus' day it was common for followers to choose their rabbi—a great teacher from whom they could learn the Law and after whom they could pattern their lives. Jesus, however, reversed the pattern. Even though Jesus' group members made choices, He was the ultimate Chooser and they the chosen ones. Let's read the following passages to see how Jesus was the ultimate Chooser.

¹³Jesus went up on a mountainside and called to Him those He wanted, and they came to Him. ¹⁴He appointed twelve—designating them apostles—that they might be with Him and that He might send them out to preach, ¹⁵and to have authority to drive out demons.
Mark 3:13-15

⁷⁰Then Jesus replied, "Have I not chosen you, the Twelve?"
John 6:70a

¹⁶"You did not choose Me, but I chose you and appointed you to go and bear fruit—fruit that will last. Then the Father will give you whatever you ask in My name."

¹⁹"If you belonged to the world, it would love you as its own. As it is, you do not belong to the world, but I have chosen you out of the world. That is why the world hates you."
John 15:16, 19

Think of a time when *you* were a chooser. How do you feel when you are the *chooser* in a situation?

How do you feel when you are the *one chosen?*

In what way are you (and the rest of the people in your small group) chosen?

On an all-star team, each member (even though he or she may come from differing backgrounds) looks at the team-mates as valuable because they have been chosen. Each team member is there to represent a cause that unites them all. How many things do you share in common with others in this group?

 ## GROWING BY DOING

Thanking the Chooser

Let's take a few minutes to pray and thank Jesus for choosing each member of our small group. He has placed us together, not by accident, but by design, so together we can build a relationship with Him and carry out His work in the world, supporting each other. What are some things you appreciate about each person in the group?

Now let's talk about our choices. Let's share why we chose to belong to this group. What does this small group community need to become for it to be a satisfying group for you? What motivated you to want to be a part of this group?

SMALL GROUP LEADER'S GUIDE

Choices

"You have a choice" is a phrase that arouses our imagination, kindles our enthusiasm, and turns on our responsibility. People come to a group with different reasons. Some choose to come because of the leader, some because of another person in the group, some because of what they will gain—information, a sense of belonging and inclusion, friends, a realm for doing what they enjoy doing. Regardless of motives, each person must make a choice to come and participate in a community called small group. However, *community* as an attitude isn't automatic—it requires time and careful handling. Having a choice in what goes in a small group builds that sense of community.

"What I invest in becomes a part of me," or as the Master Teacher reported, "Where your treasure is, there your heart will be also" (Matthew 6:21). This session's emphasis on choices provides a way to get acquainted because a person's choices reveal who that person is. It also gives opportunity to display expectations and to make an investment in a small group so that right from the beginning it becomes "our" group.

As **Group Leader** of this small group experience, *you* have a choice as to which elements will best fit your group, your style of leadership, and your purposes. After you examine the **Session Objectives**, select the activities under each heading with which to begin your community building. You have many choices.

GETTING ACQUAINTED   20–30 minutes

Pocket Principle

1 The more time group members spend sharing their lives and experiences, the sooner will be their bonding into community. At the beginning of a group, spend a great deal of time allowing members to share.

If your group is not well acquainted, take time at least to get to know one another's names before beginning this session. If the group is strong in its relational bonds, the following exercises may help to strengthen the group.

Have a group member read aloud **You Have a Choice!** Then choose one of the following activities to help create a more comfortable, nonthreatening atmosphere for the first meeting of your small group.

Birds of a Feather

Identify three distinct areas of your room as **A, B,** and **C.** Ask group members to stand and to indicate their choice among three options (See page 14) by moving to the appropriate area that represents their preference. When each choice has been made, give assembled groups two minutes to share with one another why they made that particular choice. Encourage the group to discuss the questions under each choice.

Optional—Choices and Responsibilities

Ask each group member to think of a choice he or she made

76

as a child or youth and then to share that choice and the resulting responsibility with other group members.

Optional—Pivotal Choices
Ask group members to share briefly a pivotal choice that they now see as a turning point in their lives. It could be a relationship that developed into a lifelong commitment, a career or schooling choice, a decision on where to live, or other opportunity embraced. If you have a large group (9 or more) you may want to divide into smaller groups so everyone can share in the time allotted. Give a 5 minute warning.

GAINING INSIGHT   20–25 minutes

Pocket Principle

2 The more group members talk about their understanding of how Scriptural principles relate to life, the more likely those principles are to transfer into their lives. Don't just tell; ask them to think and share.

Pocket Principle

3 The way a person participates during the first session with a group is likely to establish a pattern of participation. Help each group member respond at least once during this study to establish the habit of investing in the group.

Understanding Choices
Have group members turn to their neighbors and share at least five choices they've made today.

Scripture Study
Have group members take turns reading aloud this section as well as John 1:35-51. Then discuss the following questions.

❑ **What choices did Jesus' followers make in this passage?** (They chose to pursue Jesus, to spend time with Him, to talk about Jesus, to bring people they cared about into Jesus' presence, to obey/act on what Jesus said.)

❑ **In what ways could the disciples' choices affect the rest of their lives?** (They were attracted to Jesus, and their enthusiasm about who He was affected everything they did. Two of John the Baptist's disciples made a choice that started them [and those related to them] on an exciting experience.)

Suggest that the group think about the following question as a group member reads aloud Mark 3:13-15, John 6:70a, John 15:16, 19—**What impact do you think Jesus' words would have on the chosen disciples when they heard this?**

Discuss the following questions.

❑ **How do you feel when you are the chooser in a situation?** (Powerful, but responsible.)

❑ **How do you feel when you are the one chosen?** (Esteemed, valued, want to please the one who chose you.)

 ## GROWING BY DOING   15–20 minutes

Thanking the Chooser
As the group prays, make sure that each member is prayed for either by others in the group or by you as the leader. You may want to ask group members to divide into pairs to pray specifically for one another.

Encourage each person to share the expectations or motivations that caused him or her to want to be in this small group. It is important to know group members' agendas. After each person shares his or her reasons for wanting to be a part of the group, summarize what has been expressed.

(Small Group Session and Leader's Guide reprinted from *Let's Get Together* (GroupBuilder Resources), 8 sessions on launching a small group by Julie A. Gorman.)

EQUIPPING SESSION 5

MAY I ASK A QUESTION?
How To Develop and
Ask Good Questions

. . . .

TARGET
By the end of this session you will:

▶ Become aware of questions.
▶ Discern good questions.
▶ Learn principles for developing good questions.
▶ Feel at home with questioning in small groups.
▶ Develop skills in wording and asking questions.
▶ Be prepared for handling various responses to questions.
▶ Develop competence in effective group interaction.

MATERIALS NEEDED
Moveable chairs
Overhead projector
Blank transparencies, chalkboard, or newsprint for recording
  responses

IDENTIFYING THE ISSUE

Questions surround us. "What is your name?" "Can you tell me how I get to Bristol Street?" "How much do I owe you?" "Where's the toothpaste?" "Did you call the baby-sitter?" "What do you think about this small group?" "Do you think I talk too much?" "How do you, as a leader, make use of questions?"

Years ago there was a highly acclaimed and closely followed television game show called "The $64,000 Question." With hearts beating and breath held, thousands of viewers strained to catch the question and rooted for the contestant to come forth with the correct answer. Today the fad is to spend time pursuing "trivia questions" and people take delight in struggling over such queries as, "What was the first boxed cold cereal in America?" Every sophomore has had to recite, "To be? Or not to be? That is the question." We all know what it means to "pop the question." Jesus used questions to teach and stimulate.

"What is easier, to say to the paralytic, 'Your sins are forgiven'; or to say, 'Rise, and take up your pallet and walk?' " "Which of these three proved to be neighbor to the man who fell into the robbers' hands?" "Will you also go away?"

Brainstorm about questions for a few minutes. What do questions do? What is their value? List as many different values as you can.

Trainer's Notes

If necessary, suggest that questions can be used to: gain information, demonstrate interest, clarify, make conversation, express emotion, motivate, restate understanding, and promote interest.

Questions seem to be such a natural part of living that it would seem easy to write them and ask them. Actually, developing a good question is one of the most challenging tasks a leader can undertake. Perhaps that is due in part to the wide scope of questions. As suggested above, questions sometimes motivate you to get involved, sometimes they let a person know you understand, sometimes they can challenge to apply what you know or clarify values.

How does a leader choose questions that accomplish desired goals? How can questions be asked for maximum return? What keeps questions from being seen as interrogation? What distinguishes a relational question from an informational one or a formational one? How can a leader discern between good questions and poor questions? Can a good question be asked poorly?

EXPLORING AN IDEA
There are many guidelines for developing and asking good questions. In this session you'll focus on four which begin with **C.**

Concise. Keep your questions simple. Not obvious, but uncluttered. What are ways you can do this? Keep them short. Not, "What is the contribution and the challenge to our twentieth-century actions and attitudes of Paul's dual admonitions in Romans 12:1-2?"

Multifaceted questions appear to have been designed by a committee—everybody's unique concern included. The result is like attaching a fire hose to a garden hose nozzle. Too much is asked of one question. An overzealous or inexperienced leader, excited over numerous aspects, often tries to pack the whole study into one question rather than discriminately focusing on a manageable portion.

Usually you can tell when a question isn't concise—people look strained or confused and respond with silence or "What did you say?" Trying to be too inclusive produces a breadth that causes confusion and frustration.

Clear. Howard Hendricks is fond of saying, "A mist in the pulpit is a fog in the pew," which is another way of saying, "If a question doesn't make sense to you, it won't be clear to

83

your audience." Often you may need to reword the questions found in materials so they are clear to you—so they become a part of you. Questionnaires are worked and reworked numerous times because shared meaning is so difficult to achieve through words alone.

Words which need to be explained in order for a person to answer the question cause a question to be unclear. Sometimes a simpler word will make it clear. How would you make this question easier to understand? "What is the differentiating process Jesus uses to determine who His true disciples are?"

Sometimes a word is unclear because it has so many different definitions. Your group members will tell you they're having this problem by asking, "What do you mean by _____?" Consider the following question. What is the problem word in this sentence?

What do you project it would take for you to be successful in the next 10 years?

Be clear in your own mind about what you're trying to do with your questions. Questioning for facts may not be good for relationship building. Try a sample question in a neighbor-nudging encounter. How many ways can you ask the question below by accenting a different word?

Did I say you were stupid?

How many different emotions can you evoke? What does the questioner have in mind in each case?

Creative. Being creative doesn't necessarily mean "clever" or "unusual." A creative question has many different answers. It is *open.*

"Leading questions" are not creative. They tip you off to the answer the leader expects. "You don't think God would do that, do you?" "Don't you think you ought to follow up on

that?" These questions are weighted to insure correct response and usually reveal a questioner who cannot handle any answer apart from the projected one. This is a way to control the response.

"Guess the leader's idea" type questions cancel out creative thinking. When the leader has a certain answer in mind and everyone knows that is what counts, a guessing game is played to see who can get the "right answer" first. Here's an example of this. "What are *the three* motives behind Paul's speech?" You can change this type of question by inserting "do you think" or "some." "What do you think are some motives behind Paul's speech?"

"Limited questions" are hard to answer. The question, "How did you survive in college?" when not everyone in the group went to college, can create an uncomfortable silence. Or, "What have you learned about churches after being a member for years?" would be difficult for new Christians who haven't had that experience. "What was it like when you heard the Gospel for the first time?" There may be many in the group who can't remember or were too young to distinguish. Superlatives have a way of limiting. "What was your *best* birthday present?" "Best" is frustrating because what was "best" at one age wasn't "best" at another, or a person is afraid he or she can't remember the absolutely "best" one. Here's another example of a problem superlative: "Who is the *most* significant person in your Christian pilgrimage?"

"Yes/no" questions can be threatening. What if the responder chooses the wrong answer? Again, "What do you think" and "Why" can break this threat. For example, "Do you think there is ever a time to use yes/no questions? Why or when would they be appropriate?"

Numerous "fact questions," one after another, usually indicate a questioner who is enthralled with details for details' sake or is mechanically spitting out information without regard for meaning or linkage. Inexperienced Bible study leaders often fall into this trap because they don't have a comprehensive grasp of the material or don't understand the purpose of what they are doing. They fail to elaborate on and connect the pieces of information they seek.

Considerate. Being "considerate" means asking questions that don't embarrass the responder, that don't force him or her to reveal something negative or cause a judgmental attitude. When questions get too personal too soon, people clam up. For instance, "What is something you regret having done as a Christian?" Or, "Where are you particularly vulnerable to temptation?" Groups together for longer periods of time, where the trust level is very high, may be able to handle this level of questioning.

For new groups, sharing the past is safest. Therefore you should develop questions that call for history giving. The past is over and everyone has a history, so this feels secure.

EXPERIENCING THE INSIGHT

Collect two or three people around you by asking them a question. When you are a threesome, or more, try out on each other the questions on the Sharing Questions Worksheet below. Then talk about what makes each a good or poor question.

Sharing Questions Worksheet

Relational starter questions should be used to help group members get to know each other. Examine the following questions. How well does each work as a relational starter question? Write down any general principles that come into play as you evaluate these questions.

1. What's an area where you feel like a failure?
2. What is a prayer you are glad God didn't answer and why?
3. Share your most significant learning experience.
4. Which Pastor of this church has affected your life the most?
5. What is the contribution to the differentiating process of current educational and psychological theory and practice?
6. How do you feel about the color red?
7. What do you feel most guilty about right now?

8. What's your opinion on abortion?
9. What's one thing you like about your group and one thing you would like to improve?
10. Do you like potlucks?

EXPLORING AN IDEA

Some questions are designed to elicit information—basic facts as well as evidence of deeper understanding. These *information-seeking questions* commonly begin with phrases such as: "What is ..."; "Who was ..."; "Where are ..."; "How did ..."; "Why did ..."; or "Do you mean...."

For strong relationships to be established, group members must *bond* together. Your questions must reveal more than facts if you want to build relationships among your group members. Bonding requires that a person identify with how another feels about the facts. It means revealing emotions, personalizing facts. *Relationship-building questions* are designed to help persons reveal in a safe way who they are. They are usually found in one of these forms: "How do you feel about ... ?" "What does this mean in your life?" "When was a time when you ... ?" Look for the word *you* or *your* to be expressed or implicit in most relationship-building questions.

Application questions continue in the personal mode and may be used using an individual "you" or collective "we." To design an application question, combine words of action (e.g., do, say, write, call, give thanks) with some specific insight gained from God's Word. For example, "Now that we know _____ (insight), what is one specific way you will respond by _____ (action)?" Or, "What one change _____ (action) will knowing _____ (insight) make in your life?"

EXPERIENCING THE INSIGHT

Working in your previous cluster, work through the Kinds of Questions Worksheet. First read the Scripture passage. Then try to write three good questions that grow out of the passage. Write one for *gaining information,* one for *building a relationship* or *helping a person share,* and one for *clarifying values* or *applying the Truth.*

Kinds of Questions Worksheet

Read the following Scripture passage:

¹**Therefore, I urge you, brothers, in view of God's mercy, to offer your bodies as living sacrifices, holy and pleasing to God—this is your spiritual act of worship. ²Do not conform any longer to the pattern of this world, but be transformed by the renewing of your mind. Then you will be able to test and approve what God's will is— His good, pleasing and perfect will.**

Romans 12:1-2

From what this passage says and means, develop one of each of the three types of questions asked for below.

▶ An information question:

▶ A question for helping a person share about himself/ herself:

▶ A question for helping to apply the Truth of the passage:

EXPLORING AN IDEA

Asking questions is only the initial step. What happens when persons respond to those questions? What happens if they don't? How does a small group leader handle silence? A wrong answer? A participant's further questioning?

Silence. What do you do when no one answers? First, determine why they aren't answering. Are they just thinking—which takes time. The passage of time appears different when you are the questioner than when you are the responder. It appears to be much longer when you ask the question, and it is easy to get anxious. If you must, count to twenty, silently, to *allow enough time* for your group to think.

If they aren't answering because the question is not understood, their puzzled faces or questions about meaning will tell you that you need to *rephrase the question*. It is usually a good rule to ask the same question two different ways to help group members grasp the concept. For example, "Why do you think the Apostle Paul is stressing this principle? In other words, what is he feeling, or what has he just experienced that makes this important to him?"

Sometimes *giving an example* will help group members grasp the meaning of your question. "How does the world around us squeeze us into its mold? For instance, in our attitudes toward wrongdoing? In our attitudes toward people?"

It is also possible to act as an enabler, *calling on a specific person* to respond. But this needs to be done in a way that doesn't threaten the person. For example: "Laura, what do you think about this? What would you suggest as Paul's reason?"

Wrong Answers. When a person gives an obviously "off-the-wall" answer, there is often a stressed silence in a group. In the "Specific Answer the Teacher Is Looking for Question," some leaders will say, "No, that's not what I'm looking for." Here are several ways to respond to a wrong answer.

Take the blame for miscommunication. "I guess I didn't state that question very clearly—what I'm really asking is *(rephrase the question)*."

Give an example. "Here's an illustration of what I mean by 'pattern' in Paul. He tended to take a person or team along with him. What other patterns do you think of? For instance, patterns in *where* he ministered or *how* he ministered?"

Allow others in the group to correct by giving right answers. "Ummm. What do the rest of you think?"

Ask the person to support his or her answer. "Where do you see that in our text? How does that tie in with what we're talking about?" Many times a "wrong answer" is simply "not understood" by the leader because the whole train of thought producing it is not evident.

How Can You Respond to a Participant's Questioning? Sometimes in a group discussion, a participant will become the questioner. This can be a sign of real involvement, of digesting implications, or of honest inquiry. Be sure you understand the question being asked. One of the best ways to continue this spirit of involvement is to:

▶ *Redirect the question back to the group.* "How would you respond to John's question?" Or, "Do others of you wrestle with the same thing?"

▶ *Acknowledge the question and suggest an alternative time to pursue the answer* if the question is irrelevant, will get you off onto a tangent, is a personal problem area, or is a chronic response from a troubled person. For example, "I sense you are really concerned in asking that, Joyce. Let's talk after group about a time we could deal with it."

▶ *Give the group ownership in deciding whether or not to deal with the question right now.* "Mike's question is on a different dimension from what we've been talking about. Do you as a group want to change directions and pursue it now, or is this something Mike and I can discuss later so we can proceed in the direction we've been going?"

EXPERIENCING THE INSIGHT

```
┌─────────────── Trainer's Notes ───────────────┐
│                                                │
│  For the following case study exercise, divide the group │
│  into clusters of three.                       │
│                                                │
└────────────────────────────────────────────────┘
```

Case Study #1

You are dealing with Romans 12:1-2. You have just asked the question: "What does it mean to present your body a living and holy sacrifice?" Larry asks, "That brings up something I've often wondered about—how could God OK the sacrifice of a living person like Abraham was asked to do with Isaac?"

Your response?

Case Study #2

You are studying Romans 12:1-2. You ask, "What does this passage say about God's will for us?" Ralph says, "Well, it says that the will of God is acceptable—that means you always have to accept it, no matter what. It's kinda' like fate—what will be, will be."

Your response?

Case Study #3

Your study in Romans 12:1-2 leads you to this question: "How can we 'present our bodies' as an act of our worship?" After some time, no one has answered.

Your response?

Questions are stimulating; answers are fulfilling. God responds to His people's questions. He responds by giving them Himself and His Word. He is willing to tell you all you need to know about who He is and about how He wants you to live. Close by reading antiphonally Psalm 24:3-10, included below. Divide into two groups. One half of the group will ask the questions of the song: vv. 3, 8a, and 10a. The other half will answer them: vv. 4-6, 7, 8b, 9, and 10b.

Group 1: ³Who may ascend the hill of the LORD? Who may stand in His holy place?

Group 2: ⁴He who has clean hands and a pure heart, who does not lift up his soul to an idol or swear by what is false. ⁵He will receive blessing from the LORD and vindication from God his Savior. ⁶Such is the generation of those who seek Him, who seek Your face, O God of Jacob. ⁷Lift up your heads, O you gates; be lifted up, you ancient doors, that the King of glory may come in.

Group 1: ⁸Who is this King of glory?

Group 2: The LORD strong and mighty, the LORD mighty in battle. ⁹Lift up your heads, O you gates; lift them up, you ancient doors, that the King of glory may come in.

Group 1: ¹⁰Who is He, this King of glory?

Group 2: The LORD Almighty—He is the King of glory.
Psalm 24:3-10

EQUIPPING SESSION 6

MY, HOW YOU'VE CHANGED!
How To Help Group
Members Make Application

· ·

TARGET
By the end of this session you will:

▶ Understand what application of truth means.
▶ Realize the necessity of *practicing* truth, not just knowing it.
▶ Learn how to bring group members to a point of choosing to put truth into practice.
▶ Actually experience application in your own life.
▶ Commit yourself to helping group members change.
▶ Plan one specific way to incorporate the process of application into your own small group time.

MATERIALS NEEDED
Moveable chairs

Overhead projector
Blank transparencies, chalkboard, or newsprint for recording
responses

IDENTIFYING THE ISSUE

Sometimes being last means you get left out. If you were the last born in a fairly large family, you probably experienced the letdown of "hand-me-downs." Or did you ever rush to a free giveaway only to find that you were last and they had run out? On the other hand, some people save the "best for last." They open the biggest present at the end.

Both of these experiences can be true in your small group times. It may be, because of everything else that needs to be done, that application of the biblical principles you have discussed gets squeezed out or gets only a token amount of time at the end. However, ideally the climax of your small group time should be experienced in practicing the Truth together.

Read the following Scriptures and discuss the principles in each passage.

¹⁸And we, who with unveiled faces all reflect the Lord's glory, are being transformed into His likeness with ever-increasing glory, which comes from the Lord, who is the Spirit.

2 Corinthians 3:18

¹⁴But solid food is for the mature, who by constant use have trained themselves to distinguish good from evil.

Hebrews 5:14

⁹Jesus answered: "Don't you know Me, Philip, even after I have been among you such a long time? Anyone who has seen Me has seen the Father. How can you say, 'Show us the Father'?"

John 14:9

Second Corinthians 3:18 suggests that "we are in the process of being transformed into the likeness of Jesus." Hebrews 5:14 states that the "mature person" is one "who

94

because of practice" has his "senses trained to discern good and evil." It takes practice to become a discerning person.

God has given us opportunity to practice the Truth and He expects us to do so. Can you think of any evidences from the Scripture that Jesus expected people to change and be transformed? For instance, when Philip asked to be shown the Father, Jesus' response was "Have I been so long with you, and yet you have not come to know Me, Philip?" (John 14:9) Or consider Mark 6:52. After the disciples failed to exhibit faith in the boat on the windswept sea, Mark goes back to what had just happened in the Feeding of the Five Thousand where Jesus had shown Himself to be God, and notes "for they had not gained any insight from the incident of the loaves."

If Jesus expected persons to be different as a result of being exposed to Him and His Word, we should settle for no less. God expects more than "information collecting" when His Word is shared. As a leader you teach and enable for formation, not just information. How can you enable group members to change—to learn—as a result of interaction with biblical principles? What helps group members grow? What "principles of learning" can be put to work in your small groups? What turns a "happening" into a learning situation?

In this session you'll get an opportunity to try out learning as a learner and then examine changes within yourself.

EXPLORING AN IDEA

Unless highly motivated, we usually resist application—it means change, commitment, and work. As any beginning salesman knows, "sweaty palms" time is when you ask for a signature on the bottom line or a check to signify that a deal is closed. It's easier to stop short of that point. Larry Richards in his book, *Creative Bible Teaching*, Moody Press, has called these stopping points "Five Levels of Learning." Try them out and see what happens when you move through all five to application.

95

Write the statement below on a chalkboard or overhead transparency so you can erase or cover up certain words. Have the group read the statement together. Then erase or cover one word in the statement and call on someone to say the whole sentence including the missing word. Continue erasing and asking for a recitation of the sentence until only four or five words remain.

A rotating fragment of mineral collects no bryophytic plants.

After reading the above sentence several times, have you learned it? You didn't know the sentence before reading it, but now you know it.

This is an example of limited learning—it is called *rote*—and is the first level you reach in learning. You probably remember learning Bible verses by rote. You could say them "if you went fast enough and didn't think about what you were saying." For instance, can you remember John 3:16? You probably learned the Pledge of Allegiance and most songs by the *rote* method.

A further step in learning takes place when you can *recognize* this statement from among others. Remember how relieved you were to find out the driver's test was going to be "multiple choice" not "fill in the blanks."

Read the following examples as you discuss the *recognition principle.*

1. Don't let grass grow under your feet.
2. Moss grows on the north side of rocks.
3. A rolling stone gathers no moss.

Now translate this *recognition principle* to biblical truth. John 3:16 tells us which of the following:

1. God will get you.
2. Jesus died.
3. God sent Jesus.

It is good that you can recognize truth. This gives you a feeling of mastery. At least you can recognize right answers enough to pass the test! However, being able to identify a fact usually doesn't prompt someone to take action to change as a result of what is known.

So, on to level three where learning means being able to *restate* what a statement means.

Restate "A rolling stone gathers no moss."

This may be hard because most of us have not gone beyond rote learning of this proverb. Here are a couple of suggestions in case you're having trouble: "Being on the move — growing and changing — means you will not be in a condition to collect unwanted exterior attachments." Or, "The one who is in forward motion will not show evidence of settled stagnation."

Perhaps this is easier: restate John 3:16.

This level of learning requires a person to think harder and to comprehend more. A truth must pass through a person's mind and come out in the person's own words. But even though a person can explain what something means, that concept may not affect the individual's life. Charles Schultz has captured this idea in one of his cartoons showing Snoopy shivering in a snowstorm while Charlie Brown, warmly bundled, beneficently quotes James 2:16, "Go in peace, be warmed and be filled." Though the meaning is grasped, there is no impact of the Truth on a life situation.

Level four helps to accomplish this by exposing the various facets of a person's life that may be affected by truth. It asks, "How could this make a difference in my marriage? In my work? In my thought life? In my attitudes? In my dealing with my neighbor?"

Level four is called *relate to life*. You can see how this increases the possibilities for putting God's Truth into practice.

Consider again the "rolling stone" proverb. What are some "rolling stones" in your life that have kept you from collecting unnecessary external attachments? Or, how has constant change kept you from becoming a site for unwanted growth?

Illustrations and questions help people think of various ways a truth can affect them. For example, "I could use this truth in dealing with _____." Or, "I need to be more _____." Or, "I should try to _____." But often, the process stops there—we just *think* about how it might affect our lives. A door-to-door salesperson is not content having you think of all the ways his products could affect what you do or enhance your living. He wants you to *buy the product and use it!*

The final step to which you must bring people is to *realize* what they need to do. *Realizing* means putting something into action. For example, "What's one way this week you can practice 'rolling stone?' " Or, "What's one way you can incorporate the truth of John 3:16 in your everyday living?"

In helping persons make application of biblical truth you should think in terms of three kinds of application:

1. A change in action—I will do this, or, I will not do this.

2. A change in attitude (often expressed as an action). I will cultivate a patient attitude by reminding myself of 1 Corinthians 13:4 when I sit in a long line of traffic on the way to work this week. I will seek to develop an attitude of gratitude by thinking through specific causes for thanks at the end of my day.

3. An expression of response to God—worship, praise, or prayer—for Truth discovered.

EXPERIENCING THE INSIGHT
Suppose, after studying 1 Corinthians 12, you are convinced that God wants you to value each person in the body of

Christ, even those who are not like you. How could this be applied? (relate to life) How will you plan to actually do one of these suggestions? When? With whom? Cluster in threes to come up with one or two applications.

EXPLORING AN IDEA
Spheres of Application. There are two dimensions where application can be accomplished: right here, right now, as you practice the Truth in your small group; or out there in your life this week, but which you share with other group leaders here and now. Can you think of a way your group of three could practice application of "valuing each person in the body" right now, right here? For example, share with each in the group, "Why I'm glad you are a part of the body of Christ."

What Helps Applications? You should find the following principles useful as you begin to help your small group apply the Truth of God's Word.

1. *Understanding the Word of God.* As you study the Scripture you are laying a foundation for the application as group members grapple with what a passage means.

2. *Accepting God's Word as authority.* As you cultivate the idea that God gives His Word so that we might obey it, believe it, and prove its validity, you are developing a value for the authority of Scripture. It is not to be kept on a shelf, but tried in living.

3. *Relating it to life.* Good illustrations and questions will help group members think through ways a Truth could affect their lives, bridging the gap between principles and real-life application.

4. *Take time to practice Truth.* Applying takes time to think through and do. Allowing time for your group to do this will enable not only the application of Truth but will build this as a habit.

5. *Challenge members to be specific.* Thinking in terms of specific settings, specific persons, specific habits, helps the application to become more real and thus more likely to be put into practice. Writing it down for yourself makes it specific—not just "be a better Christian," but "ask Dan to forgive me." Or "Tell Carol how much I appreciate her standing by me in this crunch." If application isn't written, it can be shared verbally with one other. Putting intentions into words helps with following through. Sometimes a specific commitment is shared with God alone in prayer—that helps to promote follow-through also. "God, this week I want to _____."

6. *Encourage and support.* Practicing the truth together is a great encouragement. If you are convinced that you need to "encourage one another," you can do that through listening, praying, and sharing in small groups or by two's. If you cannot practice the Truth together in the group, it is encouraging to have one other person who will pray for you, and who will be waiting for a report on "how it went." That shows care.

EXPERIENCING THE INSIGHT
In units of three or four study Psalm 34:1-3. Understand what it means. Think through ways you could actually do what it says in your life. Choose one way to practice something you learned right now. Take 15–20 minutes to work through this exercise with your unit.

¹I will extol the LORD at all times; His praise will always be on my lips. ²My soul will boast in the LORD; let the afflicted hear and rejoice. ³Glorify the LORD with me; let us exalt His name together.

Psalm 34:1-3

What is something you intend to do in your small group as a result of what you have done here today?

What is one change you will implement? Share it with your group of three.

EQUIPPING SESSION 7

DO YOU HEAR ME?
How To Hear and Respond To People In Need

. . . .

TARGET
By the end of this session you will:

▶ Realize what is involved in being an effective listener.
▶ Become aware of listening barriers.
▶ Want to practice good listening skills.
▶ Learn to listen for feelings and to respond to them effectively.
▶ Recognize when to deal with a ministry need.
▶ Become conscious of ministry opportunities within a small group.

MATERIALS NEEDED
Moveable chairs
Overhead projector

Blank transparencies, chalkboard, or newsprint for recording responses

IDENTIFYING THE ISSUE

Imagine someone in your small group coming up to you and saying: "I didn't agree with what you said tonight. Maybe I just shouldn't be in this group." Or someone who says, "Why doesn't God do something about my situation? Sometimes I wonder if it pays to be a Christian." Or, "I could never do what you do. I'd make a mess of it for sure."

Being a group leader means that people will probably share with you indications that they are hurting or need someone to care. You may casually overhear conversations that reveal to you the hurts a person is experiencing. This is a good sign that they feel secure or trust you and the group with their true feelings. It may also be that they are hurting so intensely that they cannot keep from expressing that pain to others.

Listening Is a Ministry. Throughout the Psalms God is characterized as a "hearing" God who listens to His own (Psalm 86:1), whereas false idols are described in Psalm 135:17 as "having ears but hearing not." What incident comes to your mind when you think of God hearing you?

Break into pairs to share what that circumstance was and why it was so important at that point to know that God was listening.

EXPLORING AN IDEA

Learning to hear is a skill we improve with intentional practice. It takes conscious effort to focus on hearing what a person is saying. There are things that often make it hard to listen. List what some of those barriers are. Here's an example to get you started: "It's hard to listen when you have preconceived attitudes about the speaker." "Mrs. X is a chronic complainer." Or, "Mike is always trying to get attention."

You might suggest the following if they're not mentioned by anyone else:

It's hard to listen when ...

▶ You're preoccupied (e.g., with covering the lesson or with what you're going to say in rebuttal).

▶ There are distractions such as another conversation going on at the same time.

▶ You're on the defensive. (Someone says, "Working mothers create family problems," and just last week you became a working mother.)

▶ You are tired or dealing with your own issues.

▶ You are concerned with correcting their facts and logic and they are concerned with impressions and feelings. In our society we tend to value more the information level and devalue the meta-message level of talking for relationship. Deborah Tannen in her book, *That's Not What I Meant!* (Morrow, 1986), suggests that this is often reflected in gender differences. When children phone their parents they often find that the fathers want to cover the information needed and then hang up, while mothers want to continue chatting to "keep in touch." Some persons will share a tentative bit of their issues to see if you care about them personally.

▶ You trivialize a problem because it is not difficult for you.

▶ Someone speaks in a different style than you do. (You say things right out; they drop hints.)

To really listen a person must hear and clarify in order to accurately understand the other's message. That takes focused effort and usually conscious caring.

EXPERIENCING THE INSIGHT

By two's, ask each group leader to share a statement about himself or the situation. For example, "It's cold in here." The partner tries to understand what that person means by asking only yes/no questions that begin with the phrase, "Do you mean." For example, "Do you mean you feel uncomfortable?" (Yes) "Do you mean I ought to feel uncomfortable, too?" (No) "Do you want me to get you a jacket?" (No) And so on. Your goal is to get three "yes" answers and then reverse the roles with the other partner making a statement.

EXPLORING AN IDEA

Someone has said that communication is 10% information and 90% emotion. People often keep saying the same thing over and over because they don't feel that the listener has "heard" their feelings. It's not that the listener hasn't comprehended the facts, but that the feelings underlying the facts aren't heard. It's easy to jump over the feelings and begin giving advice, sharing facts, or trying to minimize the problem rather than hearing the feeling. But until a person feels that his or her feelings are heard, that person cannot "hear" facts or evaluate the situation.

Dorothy Briggs in her book, *Your Child's Self-Esteem* (Doubleday, 1970), suggests we use four common "feeling stoppers."

▶ Cheering—"It could be worse." "You'll feel better tomorrow." "You'll do fine."

▶ Reasoning—"You were able to come through worse than this in the past, so you should be able to handle this." "But God promises us that...."

▶ Judgment—"You shouldn't let yourself get this way." "As a Christian you must not feel this way."

▶ Denial—"You're not afraid (nervous, angry, depressed). Tell yourself you're feeling better (even if you aren't) and that you'll work it out."

EXPERIENCING THE INSIGHT

Now, look at the responses some persons have given when someone has been trying to tell them they were hurting. Which of these responses would tell the speaker that the listener has heard the "feelings" he or she is expressing?

	Feelings Heard	Not Heard
a. "Some people are hard to figure out."		
b. "If I were, you I'd talk to her about it."		
c. "It must be very frustrating to have something like this happen, especially when you don't know why."		
d. "We know that all things work together for good..."		

If you chose **c** above, you're hearing feelings and letting the speaker know you understand. This doesn't mean that you agree, but it signals that you do hear. And it doesn't mean that answers **a**, **b**, and **d** couldn't be given *after* the person knows that you have heard the feelings expressed. If given too soon, the person will continue to argue, trying to tell you the feeling, "Yes, I know, but I still feel like giving up." Persons need to vent feelings before they will begin to think of working through an issue.

EXPLORING AN IDEA

Persons often express feelings in terms of what they are to do. "I'm so angry I'm going to tell her, 'that's it for our relationship.'" "I'm so depressed I think I'm going to stop coming to church." We usually hear only the behavior and jump on it to try to correct it. It is very likely that the persons above will not actually do what each has declared. The extremity of the threat simply helps to express the strength of their feelings.

Reflecting feelings cultivates a climate of acceptance. When a person feels accepted, she is released from her fear of being judged. This opens the person to share more honest feelings. Knowing that you have heard him and accepted him opens a person to receive truth. Reflecting can help you find out if a person wants and needs your caring ministry. It expresses the love of Christ to another person in a unique way.

EXPLORING AN IDEA

Sometimes you must deal with ministry issues within a group and sometimes outside. But how can you know when you should set aside time in a meeting to minister to a person who is hurting and when you should deal with him outside the group?

If the issue that caused hurt concerns a happening within the group of which others are aware, it is best to deal with it in the group among those who observed it. Examples of this would include someone needing to be ministered to because of actions that happened in the course of the group's meeting.

If the situation that prompts ministry occurred outside the group and cannot be readily cared for with a brief group supportive effort, plan to meet with the hurting person separately or find someone within or outside the group with the proper helping skills to do so. This should be followed even if specifics of the circumstance were mentioned in the group. Group members cannot become problem solvers or amateur psychologists. Many issues are deep-seated and should not be shared indiscriminately.

This does not suggest that you ignore the feelings. For example, if a person is weeping, suggest, "We are aware that you seem to be feeling something painful tonight, Deborah. Would you care to share something briefly with the group or would you rather keep it to yourself and we will be supportive by praying for your comfort and healing." It may be sufficient to recognize Deborah's feelings.

If she does share, lovingly care for her in a way that feels comfortable to the members of your group. After sufficient sharing by Deborah, offer to pray for her. Above all, do not turn over the rest of the meeting to Deborah, do not allow members to give advice or to play counselor. Groups deal best with issues in which all have participated or observed the circumstances. Perhaps you, or a member of your group, know of a person experienced in helping individuals work through major issues in their lives. You might offer to help Deborah get in touch with this person.

Many who serve as leaders picture themselves as "fixers." They want to "make it right" for others and to give them the "right" answers. In fact, they fear situations where they cannot give the right answer.

More than someone to give them answers, persons who are hurting need someone to stand alongside them while they process what they already know in terms of what they are experiencing. Generally persons will do only what they have decided to do. You can be supportive but you cannot take responsibility for them and their decisions. Providing support and care help a person process into health. Beware of playing God in a person's life.

To the person in pain, advice is simply disguised criticism. It should be offered sparingly, and then only tentatively, if asked for. We cannot tell persons what to do. We can only give them guidelines under which to operate.

When you refuse to "hear" feelings, you are telling the person, "Your feelings are not OK—you have no right to feel." It's important to remember that *feelings are neither right nor wrong—what we do with them becomes a right or wrong response.*

When you "hear" a feeling and express that back to a person, it's called "reflecting." Like a mirror, you send back what has been given to you. "You are hurting because she is gone." "You feel angry and feel like you've been cheated." This does not mean that you agree with how the person feels—you are not saying right/wrong or "I feel this way too." But recognition of feelings tells a person that you hear. Then you can go on from there to help. It is interesting to see God's reflection of Cain's feelings when He observed that Cain was bent out of shape because his offering was not favored. "Why are you angry? Why is your face downcast?" (Gen. 4:5)

EXPERIENCING THE INSIGHT

Find four others who will help you with this next experience. Each person in your group of four should have a slip on which is a comment that somebody has made. Listen to the statement. Then identify what the person is feeling. What "feeling stopper" (cheering, reasoning, judgment, denial) would be natural to use here? How would that affect the person receiving it?

After identifying the feeling, try reflecting back the emotion you hear in the statement. Ask your groupmates to give you feedback.

Feeling Exercise

1. "I hate having to open up to somebody and tell them who I really am. Transparency is something I've always avoided. I think it's too dangerous to let people get too close to you. If they really know you, would they like you?"

   This person feels:

afraid	inadequate	uncomfortable	insecure
inferior	humiliated	picked on	anxious
angry	resentful		

   How could you respond to let him know you hear his feelings?

2. "I really have a hard time getting into the Word on a daily basis. I suppose I should set up some kind of system. But I've failed so often that I keep putting it off."

This person feels:

depressed   inadequate   uncomfortable   defeated
helpless   guilty   doubtful   resentful

How would you respond?

3. "I didn't agree with what you said tonight. Maybe I just shouldn't be in this group."

   This person feels:

   How would you minister to this person by responding?

4. "Why doesn't God do something about my situation?"

   This person feels:

   What would you express in response?

5. "I don't feel we are really honest in the church. We play games."

   This person feels:

What will be your response as you begin ministering?

This kind of caring is pastoral ministry at its best—one member of the body of Christ caring for another.

Often people will reveal to you only the tip of the iceberg, waiting to see if anyone picks up on their clues which seem like loud cries for help to them. Read the following piece written by an unknown author about the need to be listened to.

Could You Just Listen?

When I ask you to listen to me and you start giving me advice, you have not done what I asked.

When I ask you to listen to me and you begin to tell me why I shouldn't feel that way, you are trampling on my feelings.

When I ask you to listen to me and you feel you have to do something to solve my problem, you have failed me, strange as it may seem.

Advice is cheap; twenty cents will get you both "Dear Abbey" and Billy Graham in the same paper.

I can do for myself—I'm not helpless; maybe discouraged and faltering, but not helpless.

When you do something for me that I can and need to do for myself, you contribute to my fear and inadequacy.

But when you accept as a simple fact that I do feel what I feel, no matter how irrational, then I can quit trying to convince you and can get about this business of understanding what's behind this irrational feeling.

When that's clear, the answers are obvious and I don't
need advice.

Nonrational feelings make more sense when we understand what's behind them.

So please listen and just hear me.

And if you want to talk, wait a minute for your turn—
and I'll listen to you.

Jesus declares, "If a person has ears to hear, let that
person hear" (Mark 4:9).

In groups of five pray for one another in his or her ministry
of listening to persons who need care and understanding expressed through the ministry of small groups.

EQUIPPING SESSION 8

LET'S TALK ABOUT THAT!
How To Develop
Dynamic Discussions

. . . .

TARGET

By the end of this session you will:

▶ Become aware of what group members want in a leader.
▶ Learn what is involved in helping people interact in a way satisfying to them and to the leader.
▶ Learn skills for preparing a group for healthy discussion.
▶ Identify common responses that sabotage discussion.
▶ Learn how to respond to these saboteurs.
▶ Be motivated to care for members by exercising leadership.
▶ Demonstrate understanding of discussion leadership skills.

MATERIALS NEEDED
Moveable chairs
Overhead projector
Blank transparencies, chalkboard, or newsprint for recording responses
Envelopes with roles

IDENTIFYING THE ISSUE
Take a look at the Attribute List below. Select four items which seem most important to you leading an effective discussion time.

Attribute List

A Good Discussion Leader . . .

Can control what goes on.
Clarifies and restates ideas.
Can get everyone to talk.
Shows care for persons.
Is enthusiastic.
Practices self-disclosure (being vulnerable).
Asks stimulating questions.
Listens intently.
Explains clearly.
Helps people share their true feelings.
Is open to varied opinions and evaluations.
Can summarize thoughts and draw conclusions.

After you have chosen your "primary four" from the list, find a partner, compare choices, and discuss why you chose the four you selected.

Effective Leader Attributes. Actually, according to a study by Lieberman, Yalom, and Miles (1973), all 12 of the above attributes play a part in the four prime characteristics of the most effective leaders. Lieberman, Yalom, and Miles identified these characteristics as:

116

- ▶ Caring
- ▶ Giving meaning
- ▶ Emotional stimulation
- ▶ Executive function

Effective leaders appear to be those who are *high* in expressing the first two attributes and *moderate* in emotional stimulation and executive function.

Caring. Caring by a leader is expressed through friendliness, offering to protect the vulnerable one, supporting, and giving members encouragement and feedback along with nonjudgmentalism and praise. Effective leaders rated high in these caring attributes. But this quality, as important as it is, cannot produce a lasting positive outcome by itself.

Giving Meaning. Also necessary is the ability to give meaning, to enable understanding of ideas, procedures, and situations, and to help persons learn through development of mental structures (e.g., outlines, etc.). Effective leaders clarify concepts and explain the "whys" of what they do and what is going on among group members. This expresses respect for the person and shows effort to help the person change by first grasping what is taking place or being expressed.

Emotional Stimulation. *Moderate* use of emotional stimulation means acting so as to help persons reveal their feelings in a secure environment and at a safe pace. Not only is this effective when enabled in moderation among members, it is valued in the leader. When the leaders used sensitivity in sharing their own personal selves and asked for feedback on their leadership actions, members responded to them as to real persons and their leadership was enhanced.

Executive Function. The last quality, executive function, is expressed through organizing and setting up structures that help the group do what it is to do. Goal setting and scheduling are part of this, as are setting limits, pacing a discussion, knowing when to move on and taking action to do it. Again, this should be exercised with moderation. What do you think this quality does for group members? Why do they respond to it in a leader?

Which of these four attributes seems to be the most comfortable for you to carry out? Which challenges you?

Can you think of more times when you did some of the above actions and saw the group respond positively to your leadership?

In what ways can you, as a leader, become more effective in preparation and in the actual leading of discussions in your small group?

EXPLORING AN IDEA
Helps for Discussion. The seven steps below build effectiveness for any leader.

1. Know what to accomplish.
2. Know how long it takes.
3. Give an overview first.
4. Glue comments together.
5. Plan to involve all.
6. Encourage questions.
7. Keep it stimulating.

Step 1. Know What You Want to Accomplish. Try writing a goal for each section of your group time. For example, what is the intent of your beginning activity? What would you like to see happen as a result of your remarks? If you can do this, you become free to take the right steps to allow what you picture to happen. Scientists tell us that the human body has a marvelous capacity to balance and correct itself. Anyone knows that to carry a brimful cup of coffee across the room without spilling it, you must focus on your destination, not on the sloshing coffee. If you know that you want people to get to know and feel safe with one another (or you want them to have a feeling of investment in the group), you become free to shape and modify a discussion activity or question to cause this to happen in your group. You no longer mechanically plod through material. Your antenna pick up clues subconsciously and you add a phrase to clarify or you give an example to help people feel at ease. This is a natural adjustment that comes from knowing what you want to accomplish.

You want members of your small group to feel the freedom to self-disclose, to share the real concerns and issues they have. This freedom to ask questions and to reveal struggles they face in their sphere of living is your goal. The subject for your discussion is, "We all demonstrate and experience prejudice." What all could you do, knowing that your goal is to enable members to feel freedom to share? What would help build acceptance and trust in talking about prejudice?

Step 2. Know How Long Everything Takes. A good leader maps out a schedule and plans to be at a certain point by a certain time. There is a vast difference in an ambler and one who knows where she must be by sunset. This is an area where many leaders create a sense of insecurity as they underestimate and then exhibit a hurriedness to catch up. Such agenda anxiety often results in meanings being glossed over. Persons may go along for the ride, but they never do catch up to the real purpose. Two areas to check are:

1. Plan time to move.
2. Plan to make it easy to answer a question so time isn't wasted.

Movement into small units within the group takes time. The larger the number in the group, the longer it takes to assemble. Groups of five, six, or larger should only be attempted when the issue merits a lot of time. Reassembling that number of persons requires replacement of chairs and finding space for the "left out one," and tends to be slower in starting as each person "feels out" the situation. Pairs are effective for quick interaction and clusters work well to add dimension. Time can be saved by asking two persons to team up with the two directly behind them. Do not count off in fours unless you have a lot of time to reassemble. Grouping of any number over four requires the designation of one as leader (either appointed ahead or selected at random, e.g., "the one who ate the most for breakfast"). This eliminates the uneasy time lapse of waiting for one to volunteer.

What makes it easy to answer a question? Be sure your question is focused enough for persons to answer. Asking, "How do you feel about commitment" can take off in many directions and will use up time as persons seek to find some defining boundary. Better to ask, "In what ways have you seen commitment expressed in parenthood?" Having a question written also saves time and confusion.

Step 3. Give Listeners an Overview to Give Meaning to Your Remarks. Letting group members know ahead of time that they will be expected to discuss what you are sharing, helps them focus on your remarks and prepares them to discuss. "After we examine what God has to say about discipline, we'll do some sharing on what makes it hard or easy to be disciplined."

Explaining the kinds of activities the group will experience or why it is structured as it is helps group members feel prepared for discussion. For instance, "It is important that we hear what each person thinks and feels about this issue of submission so we feel we know each other and can relax, knowing each other's concerns. Therefore when we come to discussion we'll count on all to participate."

Step 4. Glue Your Comments Together. Sometimes it is difficult for group members to get into discussion because the previous material seems irrelevant. An effective leader builds bridges between statements and helps listeners see connections. Abrupt changes which do not seem to be relevant undermine motivation and comprehension. "We have just looked at a variety of ways in which God uses vocations to describe Himself as a worker, from the accountant to weaver. In what ways does this action of His affect the way you look at your vocation? How does God's valuing of work make an impact on your perspective of your calling?"

Step 5. Plan to Involve All. Expectation precedes action. Having an expectation that all will be involved leads to action that enables this. Again, telling people why you are asking them to be involved in any way helps them to do it. "We want to expand your relationships within this group and so we will be grouping in different ways so you can get acquainted with new people as you discuss an issue." Expect that people will respond. If they don't, clarify what you are asking and inquire whether there are any problems in doing what is asked. Remember: the key to effective leadership is letting people know why—giving them meaning. This need not be extensive, but is very important if they are to feel a part of the group and share themselves. For example, you are thinking through these steps so you can improve the effectiveness of your discussion by explaining why you lead as you do.

Step 6. Encourage People to Ask Questions. Sometimes group members feel discussion times are stilted and contrived. The leader asks; the group talks. Letting people know that their questions are equally important and inviting them to share these is key to a stimulating discussion. Your response when they do ask will let them know if you really do want their questions. You can broaden involvement by asking, "What are other questions that arise in your mind as you hear us discussing this issue?" When you think about encouraging persons in your group to ask questions, what questions come to your mind?

121

Step 7. Keep Discussion Stimulating and Exciting. Plan to include variety wherever possible. Alternate your talking with their talking. A total change of pace is needed when you sense you or the group is bored. Try a fishbowl discussion with three or four discussing a subject in the midst of the larger group. After a period of time, invite someone in the larger group to exchange seats with someone in the fishbowl and continue the discussion.

Change the groupings of members by scrambling groups. Rotate in two new persons every five minutes so that each group loses and gains two persons who have different perspectives.

Change the pace. Try popcorn brainstorming which is a rapid, nonjudgmental sharing of ideas. Or try slowing down a discussion by asking each person to spend two minutes in reflection before going on and then to share a summary statement with their group.

EXPERIENCING THE INSIGHT

You have been talking about variety so change the pace right now. Walk around the room and find another group leader who will talk with you about one of the above steps. Both of you agree on the same step. Identify how you have seen that step carried out in this equipping session. Then move on to another person and choose another step. Explore with that group leader how you have seen that step illustrated in what you have been doing here. Take 10 minutes for this exercise. Then find out who took the most steps (i.e., discussed the greatest number with others in the 10 minutes).

IDENTIFYING THE ISSUE

Now spend a few minutes discussing some of the "hazards of discussions" and how to overcome them. List the hazards you have encountered or envisioned. Place these on display and be sure all are discussed by the time you finish this session.

EXPLORING AN IDEA

───────── Trainer's Notes ─────────

Select two or three group members, preferably experienced group leaders, who will prepare ahead of time to help communicate information and skills in this section. Before this equipping session, talk through potential suggested hazards of discussion and how to overcome them. Hand out copies of the hazards worksheet. Discuss each question, asking your "discussion doctors" to prescribe a cure after you have described the "discussion disease." To guide your discussion, some suggested answers to each question are listed following the worksheet below. Plan to deal with as many of these hazards as you can so group leaders feel equipped with skills and ideas for overcoming them.

Hazards of Discussion Worksheet

Five Deadly Diseases of Small Group Discussion
1. What do I do with a group where I continually get negative responses?

2. What can I do with those who dominate the discussion?

3. What do I do if I have opposing opinions?

4. What if persons in the group look to me as leader to answer everything?

5. What do I do with interruptions to discussion where persons use discussion opportunities to clown or go off on tangents?

Use the following guide as an aid to the discussion of each question.

1. Negative persons tend to be very vocal. Rather than giving them "open season" in your group, break your group into smaller units with one to report from each. This may nullify the negative individuals or at least, reduce their influence. Also listen for identifying clues as to why these persons are negative. For instance, your negative member(s) may: be present but not want to be (spouse forced them to come); be trying to cover up his fears, too many ideas and changes are threatening to his security; have developed years of bitterness from low self-esteem; want attention. Try to develop a design that will respond to these core needs.

2. Again, creating small groups within the group limits the scope of the domination. Utilizing a "fishbowl" where persons in a center circle discuss while those in an outer circle listen, allows you to select the inner group who speak. Try looking away from a dominator so attention is not focused on him. Try sitting beside a dominator. The lack of eye contact that occurs when someone sits beside the leader often tones down their response. Use phrases like, "How do these things sound to those of you who haven't said anything?" "Are there other comments or opinions?" Take time to ask participants how they feel about your discussion times. Hand out reactions sheets that allow people to register anonymously such items as, "Do you get to say as much as you like?" "What word describes our discussion times?" "What would you suggest to improve our discussions?"

3. Actually, this can be stimulating if you see "difference" as

a positive. Each party probably sees some aspect of truth hidden from the other, so together they increase the whole. Seek to find points of agreement and strengths in each. Keep the focus on the issue and ideas, not on the person. Don't say "John's idea" and personalize the concept so that John's self-esteem is wrapped up in defending the issue. Instead say, "the idea that was presented by John" or identify it by some fact in the idea (e.g., "the lordship salvation concept" versus the "salvation by faith stance"). It may be wise to leave with two opposing conclusions. You can summarize, "Some of us feel most strongly about the people in this situation and others of us accentuate the commitment. Both are valid views."

4. While this condition can be most flattering, the group dependency can become oppressive and keeps them from maturing. Throw their questions back to the group for resolution. If answered by another, do not add your "two cents" so you have the last word. Sometimes, dividing into participatory units causes them to come up with thoughtful solutions. "That's a good question. Share with the person beside you your opinion on that." Or, "What do you think you could do about that?" Doing a role play that stops before solving an issue can motivate and involve persons in thinking through how each would handle the concern. Ask half the group to be "consultants" to the other half. If your group is dependent on you for the "right answers," ask yourself why that is occurring. Do they need less "expert lecturing," more specific commendation to build their confidence? Less quick rescuing by the leader and more wrestling personally before coming to conclusion? Which of your leader behaviors may need to change?

5. Sometimes it is helpful to set up a "referee" who reminds the group when they are getting off target. This needs to be agreeable to the group and should be a person with enough confidence to speak up if it is to be successful. Agreeing to set aside time (2–3 minutes) right after discussion for the interrupter sometimes alleviates the situation. For example, "That's an interesting comment, Bob. We'll get back to that in a minute." Or, "Charlie, you are gifted in making us laugh.

How about we give you three minutes at the end of our discussion to "show us your stuff"?

Giving each person a copy of the question to be discussed or even breaking down the question to more specific questions helps those people who seem to have a hard time grasping and staying within boundaries. For example, "What is hard about being a man in today's world? What expectations from the media make it difficult? What from the job world colors how people look at men's roles? What in the changing role of women affects this male role?" Any of these questions make more clear the first question.

Listen to what is throwing off the discussion. Are the directions not clear? Does an idea need to be broken down? Is the same person always acting out a need for attention? Do you need to give examples so persons who learn in different ways can understand what you are saying?

EXPERIENCING THE INSIGHT

Divide into units of four or more for a roleplay. Discuss this question: What experiences have you had with discussions, and what have you learned that you could pass on?

Trainer's Notes

Give each foursome an envelope containing slips of paper on which are written roles to be assumed in the group. One person should receive the role of leader, another should receive one of the following roles: Negative Dominator, Opposer, Dependent, Interrupter who switches to tangent. Blank slips indicate the person is to be himself or herself. The "hazard person" should subtly present his or her view while playing the role assigned; others in the group must recognize the role and seek to overcome it. Take 10–15 minutes to try this experience.

As you end this session, examine the discussion Moses had with God in Exodus 33:12-23. Look for one principle that helped make this a positive discussion situation that you can share with your group. For instance, both Moses and God give evidence of really listening to one another. What other aspects enriched this discussion? How does this picture of God as "Discusser" encourage you as you think of talking with Him?